Gigged

'Sarah Kessler's wonderful book offers unprecedented illumination of the promise, and the peril, of the gig economy by taking a deep and intimate dive into the day-to-day lives of the workers who rely on it. The resulting insights are important and often troubling.'

Martin Ford, author of *The Rise of the Robots*

'With deep reporting and graceful storytelling, Sarah Kessler reveals the ground truth of a key part of the American workforce. Her analysis is both astute and nuanced, making *Gigged* essential reading for anyone interested in the future of work.'

Daniel H. Pink, author of *Drive*

'Kessler goes behind the statistics to tell the stories of people making a living (sometimes just scraping by) as gig economy workers. *Gigged* is smart, entertaining, moving, and at times even inspiring. Sarah Kessler writes like a dream. If you want to know how work is changing and how you too must change to keep up, you must read this book.'

Dan Lyons, author of *Disrupted*

'In this well-researched and beautifully written book, Sarah Kessler provides a very accessible but sophisticated analysis of the "gig economy". While vividly telling moving stories about individual hardships and achievements, it provides a broad perspective that helps us see the gig economy as the latest manifestation of the long-running historical struggle over power, security and risk between different classes. It is essential reading for anyone who is interested in understanding the future of our economy and society.'

Ha-Joon Chang, author of
23 Things They Don't Tell You About Capitalism
and *Economics: The User's Guide*

Gigged

THE GIG ECONOMY, THE END OF
THE JOB AND THE FUTURE OF WORK

SARAH KESSLER

BUSINESS
BOOKS

1 3 5 7 9 10 8 6 4 2

Random House Business Books
20 Vauxhall Bridge Road
London SW1V 2SA

Random House Business Books is part of the Penguin Random House group of companies
whose addresses can be found at global.penguinrandomhouse.com.

First published by Random House Business Books in 2018
First published in the United States by St Martin's Press in 2018

www.penguin.co.uk

A CIP catalogue record for this book is available from the British Library.

ISBN 9781847941732

Printed and bound by Clays Ltd, St Ives plc

Penguin Random House is committed to a sustainable future for
our business, our readers and our planet. This book is made from
Forest Stewardship Council® certified paper.

For my family:
Debra, Steve, Richard,
and Alex

Contents

PART III

Fine Print

PART IV

Backlash

PART V

The Future of Work

Preface

When I first heard about the "future of work" in 2011, I was working as a reporter at a tech blog—a job that involved wading through an endless stream of startup pitches.

This future, dozens of young entrepreneurs explained to me, didn't involve jobs. Nobody liked jobs: The boredom! The rigid structure! The obedience! What the world really needed were gigs.

The pitch came in different versions. Some startups had created ecommerce stores for labor. Small businesses and Fortune 500 companies alike could sift through worker profiles by skill and hire them on a project-by-project basis. Other startups worked more like dispatchers. Drivers, dog walkers, and errand runners could get notifications on their phones when a job became available and choose to either accept it or reject it. A small handful of companies had taken a third approach, breaking work into tiny tasks that took only minutes and paid only cents. They assigned online crowds of people to work on large, tedious projects, like transcribing audiotapes, or checking to make sure that grocery stores across the country remembered to put a certain brand of cola in a prime location.

The rise of these new apps, their founders assured me, meant that soon we would all be working on the projects we chose, during the hours that we wanted. We would no longer be laboring for the man, but for our own tiny businesses. This meant that in the future, it wouldn't matter how many jobs got shipped overseas or were taken by robots. We could work for our neighbors, connect with as many projects as we needed to get by, and fit those gigs in between our band rehearsals, gardening, and other passion projects. It would be more than the end of unemployment. It would be the end of drudgery.

The idea was deeply appealing to me. In addition to sounding like more fun than a job, this version of the future of work relieved a deep uncertainty I had about the future.

From a young age, my baby boomer parents had instilled in me that the mission of becoming an adult—the path to dignity, security, and independence—was to obtain a job. Most adults I knew in my rural Wisconsin town had a straightforward profession like teacher, lawyer, or mechanic. They worked at the grocery store or for the postal service. A large Nestlé factory in a town nearby made the air smell like chocolate if the wind blew just right, and another factory made Kikkoman soy sauce. Becoming employable—not following dreams, seeking some sort of personal fulfillment, or whatever it is they tell kids in coastal states—was in itself deserving of respect and dignity.

So eager was I to become a real person, a person with a job, that I'd spent a good chunk of my summer vacation before high school at a greenhouse, picking aphids off of herbs and pulling the hard-to-reach weeds (being 13, I was skinny enough to squeeze between plant stands). My parents didn't need the money. I didn't need the money. Jobs just felt instinctively important.

I'm told most millennials don't feel that way, but I haven't really met many people in general who don't value stability and safety. Maybe what makes millennials different is that those things feel particularly elusive. My peers and I came of age at a time when everything everyone believed about work was at best in flux and at worst already clearly no longer the case.

In 2005, when I was a junior in high school, I decided I would become a journalist. In 2007, as newsrooms were scrambling to move their business models online, the Great Recession started. And three years after that, the winter of my senior year of college, the unemployment rate in the United States hit double digits. Only the computer programmers, it seemed, were excited for graduation. As I conjured a frantic storm of resumes, informational interviews, and job fair mailing lists, I had trouble sleeping and, at times, breathing. Though at the time I was narrowly focused on my own employment prospects (or lack thereof), my anxiety was small by comparison to many. I had a college degree, parents willing to help me, and connections at a local greenhouse that would have been happy to have me back for another summer. I was going to be ok. About the future, the world around me, I wasn't so sure.

Media wasn't the only industry being remade by technology. As newsrooms were announcing layoffs, other companies were using internet freelance marketplaces and staffing agencies to zap white-collar jobs overseas. Artificial intelligence and robotics were replacing others. Many of the jobs that remained in the United States no longer came with security. Companies had, under pressure from shareholders, cut the fat from their benefits packages for employees, piling more and more risk onto their shoulders. As the economy recovered, the companies hired temp workers, contract workers, freelancers, seasonal workers, and part-time workers, but full-time jobs that had been lost to the recession were never coming back. Between 2005 and 2015, nearly all of the jobs added to the US economy would fall into the "contingent" category.[1] That "job" that we'd all been told was the key to our secure life no longer seemed like a natural path.

As a young person, you're not allowed to sit out the future. You don't get to put off learning how to use email because you'd rather fax. Nobody thinks that's endearing. When you see a trend coming down the pike, you know it's going to hit you. So perhaps when entrepreneurs described for me a world in which work would be like shopping at a bazaar (a gig economy startup had picked up this concept in its name, Zaarly), it appealed to me more than it would have to someone with more gray hairs: I'll take that vision of the future—no need to play that horrifying mass unemployment and poverty vision that I had all lined up and ready to go.

I wrote my first story about the gig economy in 2011, long before anyone had labeled it the "gig economy." The headline was "Online Odd Jobs: How Startups Let You Fund Your-self."[2] Though my job changed throughout the next seven years, my fascination with the gig economy didn't. I first watched as the gig economy became a venture capital feeding frenzy, a hot new topic and a ready answer to the broader economy's problems. Then, as stories of worker exploitation emerged, I listened as the same companies that had once boasted about creating the "gig economy" worked to distance themselves from the term. I saw the gig economy start a much-needed conversation about protecting workers as technology transforms work.

The more I learned, the more I understood that the startup "future of work" story, as consoling as it was, was also incomplete. Yes, the gig economy could create opportunity for some people, but it also could amplify the same problems that made the world of work look so terrifying in the first place: insecurity, increased risk, lack of stability, and diminishing workers' rights. The gig economy touched many people. Some of them were rich, some poor, some had power, and some didn't. Its impact on each of them was different.

The chapters of this book alternate between five of their stories. It's not intended to be a complete, bird's-eye view of the gig economy. Any economy is built by humans, and this book is about them.

PART I

THE END OF THE JOB

CHAPTER 1

A VERY OLD NEW IDEA

AT SOUTH BY SOUTHWEST 2011, THE NAPKINS FEATURED QR codes. Flyers rained down from party balconies, and the grilled cheese—provided by group messaging app GroupMe— was free.

Startups looked forward to the tech-focused "Interactive" portion of the famous music festival in Austin, Texas, like a popular high school student looks forward to the prom. One of the new companies among them, it was widely assumed, would be crowned a "breakout hit," just as Twitter had once "broken out" by introducing its app to the tech-savvy SXSW crowd. It was only a matter of attracting enough attention— an effort that usually involved a marketing gimmick.

At the time, Uber was a little-known app that worked as a dispatch service for local owners of licensed private car companies. Its attempt at guerrilla marketing was an on-demand pedicab service.

The startup decorated 100 rented pedicabs with banners that said "I U" next to a solid black shape of Texas ("I Uber Texas," I suppose), and in interviews with bloggers, its executives hopefully suggested that riders post photos of themselves with the hashtag #Uberspotting. "If you're an Uber virgin, prepare to experience the future of transportation," its blog explained, helpfully noting that the process of calling an Uber pedicab would be easy to navigate "even when drunk."

Within a few short years, Uber would become one of the most valuable companies in the world. It would allow anyone—not just the professional drivers with which it had begun—to earn money as a taxi driver, and its fares (then $15 at minimum) would drop so low that in some cities they'd compete with public transportation. The startup would raise more than $12 billion in venture capital funding at a valuation that made it, on paper, worth more than 100-year-old companies like GM and Ford, and the Uber business model would give rise to an entire category of startups. The transportation service would also set a new expectation among consumers: that everything should come to them "on demand," at the push of a button—an idea that would reshape service industries, retail, and digital interface design.

But at SXSW 2011, Uber just looked like yet another dream.

At the time, I was working as a reporter at a tech blog. My list of "13 Potential Breakout Apps to Watch at SXSW 2011,"[1] published the week before the festival, featured four group messaging apps, an app that turned a cell phone into a walkie-talkie (because I somehow thought walkie-talkies were better than phones?), and two nearly identical photo-sharing apps (one of which was Instagram). Uber didn't make the cut.

I wasn't alone in ignoring Uber. Despite its earnest attempt at social media marketing, only about five of SXSW Interactive's nearly 20,000 attendees that year participated in #Uber-spotting.

Uber attracted nearly as little attention a year later with an offer to deliver barbecue to SXSW attendees. The hype that year instead surrounded an app called Highlight, which made phones buzz when strangers in the same proximity had mutual friends and interests, as determined by their social media accounts. "The way we find people has been terribly inefficient," Highlight's founder told me earnestly in an interview.[2] "We don't realize how horrible it is because it's always been that way." He was dead serious about human interaction being broken, and his pitch for fixing it with an app was quite effective. The Highlight hype became so pervasive that at one panel I attended, a waggish moderator instituted a fake drinking game: "Every time Highlight is mentioned, drink twice . . . and then punch yourself." Nobody, by contrast, was talking about Uber.

I had so little expectation of Uber becoming a mainstream utility that when I took my Uber-sponsored pedicab ride, I used my work email address to sign up for the app. I didn't want my personal email account to get spam.

It wasn't for another two years, by which time Highlight had been all but forgotten, that Uber finally emerged as a darling of Silicon Valley. Its "breakout" had nothing to do with a marketing stunt.

In 2013, the company raised a $258 million round of funding led by Google's investment arm, Google Ventures—an amount that Gawker's tech blog called "stupefying."[3]

The $258 million investment seemed remarkable partly because Uber had so little in common with the hot apps of the time, those for sharing photos, turning phones into walkie-talkies, or making social connections on the street. Though some of these "potential breakout apps" sound trivial or silly in retrospect, they all had the potential to become quickly and massively profitable—Instagram and Snapchat both emerged from this period—which isn't the case for most companies. By the time Facebook bought Instagram, the most successful of my "2011 breakout apps," for $1 billion in 2012, the photo-sharing service had 30 million users but only 13 employees, including its cofounders. That's more than $75 million of value per person.

Venture capitalists love companies that scale massively with as little infrastructure as Instagram. They generally ignore companies that grow slowly and sustainably over time, which, until around 2013, included most companies that sold in-person services like transportation.

Uber, though, was changing the game. Instead of buying cars or hiring employees, it made two apps: one for customers, one for drivers. When a customer requested a ride, Uber sent a notification to a nearby driver, who used his own car to do the job. Uber handled payments and charged a commission. All it needed to grow was the same thing that Instagram needed to grow: app downloads. The startup had figured out how to scale an analog service company as though it were a software company.

Uber avoided medallions, special license plates, and other government-created systems aimed at regulating taxi and limousine companies by claiming that it was a technology company rather than a transportation company. This would soon cause a dramatic confrontation between itself and regulators. But another key to the startup's seemingly endless potential for growth was—as important, powerful things so often are—extremely boring, at least at surface level. It was essentially a tax classification.

Uber had called its drivers "independent contractors." This relieved the company from government-mandated employer responsibilities in most countries, and in the United States, where Uber started, it relieved the company of almost all of them. Workers who are classified as "employees" must be paid while they take coffee breaks and must be treated according to anti-discrimination laws. They come with commitments to contribute to government safety net programs for retirement and unemployment benefits. And they can be difficult to fire when business circumstances change.

Independent contractors come with none of these responsibilities. They also do not have the right to unionize under US federal collective bargaining laws, and there's no requirement to provide them with training, equipment to do the job, or benefits.[4] The situation is similar, albeit to a lesser extent, elsewhere. UK employers, for instance, do not need to offer sick days, holiday pay, a guaranteed minimum wage, or other benefits to self-employed contractors.

When a driver signed up to work for Uber as an independent contractor, he or she (but most likely he, as 81% of US drivers, as of December 2015, were men[5]) supplied his own car, gas, and overly pungent air fresheners. He paid for his own coffee breaks and his own health insurance. All of the responsibility of being in business, including taxes, rested on his shoulders. An Uber driver, in other words, was as close to a piece of code as Uber could find without having the cars drive themselves (an initiative that quickly became the company's priority).

It seemed to investors like a smart strategy, but it wasn't a new one. Decades before Uber started, companies in Silicon Valley had begun shifting work to independent contractors, subcontractors, and temporary workers as a way to reduce cost and liability. As an ad for the temporary staffing agency Kelly Services put it in 1971, the type of worker clients could expect to hire through such an agency:

Never takes a vacation or holiday.

Never asks for a raise.

Never costs you a dime for slack time. (When the
   workload drops, you drop her.)

Never has a cold, slipped disc or loose tooth. (Not on
   your time anyway!)

Never costs you for unemployment taxes and Social
   Security payments. (None of the paperwork,
   either!)

Never costs you for fringe benefits. (They add up to
   30% of every payroll dollar.)

Never fails to please. (If your Kelly Girl employee
   doesn't work out, you don't pay.)[6]

By 2009, the year Uber launched, nearly all taxi drivers and around 13% of the US population were already self-employed or working as independent contractors. Other alternatives to hiring employees were also on the rise. Around 45% of accountants, 50% of IT workers, and 70% of truck drivers were working for contractors rather than as employees at the companies for which they provided services.[7] And the number of temp workers in the United States was on its way to an all-time high. By 2016, 20% to 30% of the working-age population in the United States and European Union had engaged in freelance work.[8] Add part-time work to the mix, and some estimates put the percentage of the US workforce that did not have a full-time job as high as 40%.[9] Uber merely took a trend among corporations—employing as few people as possible—and adapted it for the smartphone era.

The Uber model worked great for both venture capitalists and customers. Uber's technology was inarguably a huge improvement over the incumbent system for hailing a ride (which in an era of online shopping and dating apps somehow still involved raising a hand and hoping a cab would pass). Several months after Uber confirmed the massive Google Ventures investment, data about its users leaked to the press. They showed that around 80,000 new customers were signing up for Uber every week (about as many new users as Instagram added per week in late 2010) and suggested the company was on track to make around $210 million by the end of the year.[10] Success seemed inevitable.

While any successful startup spawns imitators, with Uber,

it felt like a gold rush. Entrepreneurs and venture capitalists suddenly wanted to apply the Uber business model to every analog industry that had once seemed too slow for Silicon Valley.

If SXSW was the high school prom of the startup world, *TechCrunch* was its cheerleader. The tech blog trumpeted each "Uber for X" app's arrival with headlines such as:

**POSTMATES AIMS TO BE
THE UBER OF PACKAGES—AND MORE**

WOULD YOU USE AN UBER FOR LAWNCARE?

**BLACKJET, THE UBER OF PRIVATE JETS,
RELEASES ITS IPHONE APP**

SO I FLEW IN AN "UBER FOR TINY PLANES"

**MEET STAT, THE STARTUP THAT WANTS
TO BE UBER FOR MEDICAL TRANSPORT**

Startups made Uber for food. Uber for alcohol. Uber for cleaning. Uber for courier services. Uber for massages. Uber for grocery shopping. Uber for car washes. Even Uber for weed. Uber itself hinted that it would take its business model far beyond transportation: "Uber is a cross between lifestyle and logistics," Uber CEO Travis Kalanick told *Bloomberg*. "Lifestyle is *gimme what I want and give it to me right now* and logistics is physically delivering it to the person that wants it . . . once you're delivering cars in five minutes, there's a lot of things you can deliver in 5 minutes."[11] The presumption was that because Uber's business model worked for calling cars, it could work for any other service, too.

By the end of 2013, 13 startups that described themselves as "Uber for" something had raised venture capital, according to *TechCrunch*'s funding database. And by 2014, *New York Magazine* would count an astounding number of "Uber for X" startups—14 separate companies—in the laundry category alone.

Eventually the true independence of the micro-entrepreneurs these businesses relied upon would be challenged in court; workers who felt exploited rather than emancipated by on-demand labor would complicate an otherwise utopian narrative; and what became known as the "gig economy" would attract attention to the ways in which the rest of the economy was unprepared for the future of work.

But at the height of "Uber for X," few people in the startup world batted an eye. As the then-CEO of the odd job–marketplace TaskRabbit put it, the gig economy was on track to "revolutionize the world's labor force."[12]

CHAPTER 2

NO SHIFTS. NO BOSS. NO LIMITS.

BY THE END OF 2014, UBER HAD LAUNCHED IN PARIS, Sydney, and London, and its momentum was so strong that *Fast Company* ran a story headlined "How Uber Conquered the World."[1] The five-year-old startup was launching in a new city nearly every other day. Not just in global cities, but in Flint, Michigan; Milwaukee, Wisconsin; and Salt Lake City, Utah—places where cabs have never been prevalent.

Because Uber had few brick-and-mortar offices and no cars, what it launched in each city was essentially a marketing campaign that targeted two distinct audiences: drivers and riders. To the latter, Uber offered free rides—as many as a full two weeks-worth in Kansas City, Missouri, and up to 20 rides in Salt Lake City, Utah—and it partnered with local celebrities, in one case inviting Brandon Knight, a basketball star in Milwaukee, Wisconsin, to take the first ride in that city.

To drivers, it sold an idea that was even more powerful than free stuff, which it summarized on a billboard strategically posted near the Taxi and Limousine Commission's office in New York City: "No shifts. No boss. No limits."

These six words embodied the basic pitch with which virtually every gig economy company would lure workers in the years that followed. Freedom from the tyranny of the punch clock, the autocratic boss, the finite wages and limited opportunities of the 9-to-5 job. Driving for Uber meant that you were *free*. Not only free, but an *entrepreneur*.

The company didn't rely merely on billboards to spread the message. It set up an affiliate marketing program. Drivers earned a bonus, usually around $200, if they recruited a friend, a bonus structure that would soon become standard elsewhere in the gig economy.[2] For some, these bonuses were another appealing aspect of the job. Workers could use them to simultaneously supplement their income from fares *and* position themselves to others as small business owners, entrepreneurs, and members of the tech class. For a nominal cost, Uber had created a remarkably enthusiastic salesforce.

That's how Mamdooh Husein became an Uber driver.

A 28-year-old waiter in Kansas City whose mother and everyone else calls "Abe," he was initially skeptical when one of his coworkers told him about the ride-hailing app. Abe had lived in Kansas City for most of his life, and he had never once had an occasion to take a cab. He couldn't see how what was essentially a taxi business could work in the city, or how his friend could make the $500 per weekend in profits that he'd reported. He wanted a demonstration.

After work, Abe and his de facto recruiter drove to Kansas City's main street—a modern downtown strip that looks like an outdoor shopping mall—and turned on the Uber app.

Almost immediately, Uber started routing jobs to the phone, pinging as though golden coins were being collected in a video game.

Maybe Uber wasn't a scam after all, thought Abe. He would know, as he had fallen for scams before. Most recently, he'd spent thousands of dollars on a pyramid scheme that had promised to help him become a millionaire.

In 2009, he joined a club created by Kevin Trudeau, a famous TV pitchman and the author of a series of books that includes *Natural Cures "They" Don't Want You to Know About* and *Recession Cures "They" Don't Want You to Know About* (there were "debt cures," "free money," and a "weight loss cure" that "they" didn't want you to know about, too). The Trudeau secret that ultimately sent Abe into a financial tailspin was a 14-CD audio lecture called *Your Wish Is Your Command: How Anyone Can Make Millions.*[3]

Trudeau advised listeners that they could become millionaires by joining an elite network of individuals that Abe believed included the president of the United States. It bore an impressive name with an intoxicating acronym—the Global Information Network (GIN). At the top of GIN, Trudeau explained, were people in the "inside circle" who ran the show. At the bottom were lowly non-millionaires, those paying to gather the information they needed to advance through "levels." Advancing through these levels, of course, required recruiting others to the club. And recruiting others to the club involved selling them "tools," mostly audiobooks, to educate them about GIN and the law of attraction.

Abe didn't have a girlfriend or many close friends. He'd been raised by a Muslim stepfather and a Christian mother, and he had, on his stepfather's insistence, been strictly religious growing up—fasting (or at least pretending to fast) during Ramadan and getting up early to pray. Since rejecting Islam, he had spent less time with his parents. The house Abe lived in, which he told me he had purchased after saving for years, felt almost as empty as his life. It contained little furniture, aside from an elaborate security setup ("I live in the hood," Abe said). He was frugal to the point that he slept on an air mattress.

GIN fed Abe's ambition and told him that he could be rich and important, without laboring through new education or taking orders from managers who made him feel small. Among its lessons, it advised listeners to follow the "law of attraction," which involved the same philosophy promoted by the mega-bestseller *The Secret*: that thinking positive or negative thoughts brings positive or negative experiences into one's life. That by believing something, you make it happen.

Abe strove obsessively to join GIN's inside circle. To make it look like he'd met his goal, he signed up fake people, paying special "reduced" promotion fees of $150 on their behalf.

The inner circle, though, never materialized. As one judge would eventually put it, Trudeau was "deceitful to the core."[4] False claims he made while marketing another best-selling book, *The Weight Loss Cure "They" Don't Want You to Know About*, which encouraged readers to eat just 500 calories per day, would ultimately result in a $37 million penalty from the FTC and a ten-year prison sentence. GIN, it would eventually be revealed, was a $110 million pyramid scheme that had scammed 35,000 members.

After GIN, Abe found himself deeper in debt. By his own estimation, he hadn't paid back any credit in ten years. In the years after he joined the club, he was sued for debt. He failed to pay his taxes, and a lien was placed on his house. All of which helps explain why he was cautious about new business opportunities.

The Uber pitch felt disturbingly familiar to Abe. The company's marketing suggested that he could become financially independent—an entrepreneur rather than a mere worker— and induced him to recruit friends.

Uber had created a Delaware-based subsidiary for subprime auto loans, Xchange Leasing, which in 2015 advertised "ALL CREDIT LEVELS ARE ELIGIBLE TO APPLY," in all caps. After drivers signed up, the company would deduct their weekly car payments directly from their Uber earnings.[5] In New York, Uber for years referred drivers to dealers who offered similar subprime loans (the company has since shut down Xchange Leasing and ended its subprime car leasing program in New York).[6] As it recruited new drivers, the startup could sound a lot like a persistent pitchman for these financing options. A potential driver who had submitted his phone number to Uber could, for instance, expect a string of text messages like this real example from New York City:

Monday 8:28 AM

Get started this week! Your next step is to make an appointment to visit the Uber office. Earn $6,000 in your first month—GUARANTEED.

Monday 12:09 PM

Still need a wheelchair accessible vehicle (WAV) class before renewing your license? Schedule a FREE morning, afternoon, or evening class.

Tuesday 9:51 AM

New/Used vehicles for rent & lease-to-own from Fast Track Leasing! NEW SPECIAL OFFERS.

Wednesday 8:02 AM

Your next step is to make an appointment to visit the Uber office. Get started today & earn $6,000 in your first month—GUARANTEED.

Thursday 9:25 AM

Ready to start driving? Come visit us at our new location to get started!

Friday 8:02 AM

There is no better time to start driving! Make $6k in
your first month—GUARANTEED.

Friday 11:23 AM

Get started this weekend! Book a rental with Buggy
TLC Rentals this weekend & get $50 off your 1st week
from Buggy.

Uber pitched aggressively, set lofty expectations, and encouraged drivers to invest money in renting or leasing a car up to its standards. It made promises that were sometimes hard to believe. But as Abe drove around Kansas City with his coworker, and the app continued to ping with real ride requests from real people, he started to believe that it really was a great opportunity.

"I started seeing pings left and right," Abe remembers. "I started saying, wow, there are a lot of people who use the service. Maybe there is some money to be made." Later that week, Abe signed up.

People have long dreamed of escaping the rigidity and conformity of their jobs. But the pitch that Uber used to recruit drivers—independence, flexibility, and freedom—seemed especially well suited to the preferences of a new demographic that had become the object of fascination, even obsession, for virtually every marketer, trend spotter, and sociologist concerned with generational shifts: the millennial.

Survey-taking millennials have ranked personal development and flexibility above cash bonuses; stated higher expectations for working their own hours; and have rated work-life balance as more essential than any other job quality, including positive work environment, job security, and interesting work.

These types of findings (often best read in the voice David Attenborough uses to narrate wildlife documentaries) have led to widespread accusations that millennials ("a fascinating species") are conspiring to upend the workplace: "The 9 to 5 job may soon be a relic of the past, if Millennials have their way," begins one column from *Forbes*.[7] Another, from the *New York Times*, asks, "Are millennials—those born from roughly 1980 to 2000—about to fundamentally change companies for the better? Yes, if companies dare to listen."[8] The *Washington Post* framed the same idea a bit more cynically: "This pampered, over-praised, relentlessly self-confident generation . . . is flooding the workplace," its columnist wrote. "They'll make up 75 percent of the American workforce by 2025—and they're trying to change everything."[9]

But the survey results that suggested millennials thought about work in a drastically different way than their parents weren't exactly a mystery. Let's pretend you're a millennial (unless you are, like the largest segment of the American work-force, actually a millennial, in which case you can just be yourself).[10] Now, do you like flexibility and freedom at work?

You do! It's not exactly a shocking result. But compared to previous generations of young people who might have also desired more independence, you, a millennial with professional skills, can more easily discard your full-time, traditional job—thanks to the internet.

There's a classic economic explanation for this:[11] People de-cide to join law firms, medical practices, and other compa-nies, rather than sell their skills directly, when the cost of doing business—making sales, handling finances, communicating with customers—is higher than the bump in pay they might receive by striking out on their own. With the internet, many of these costs have become lower or even disappeared. Few people need a receptionist if they have voicemail and an email inbox (and those who do can hire a virtual personal assistant for around $5 an hour). Software programs handle book-keeping, and for many professionals, working online negates the need to rent an office.

Earning an income without a traditional job simply doesn't require as big an investment as it once did. And as gig econ-omy platforms began to focus on all sorts of white-collar pro-fessions, they helped clear one of the last big obstacles to working independently: a way to find work. The idea of inde-pendent work is appealing whether you are young or old, and though the gig economy is often portrayed as an invention of the young, both demographics joined. Between 46% and 60% of young people in Europe and the United States do some type of independent work, but they make up only about a quarter of the independent workforce.[12]

Curtis Larson, a 24-year-old programmer living in New York City, is one of them.

Before Curtis joined the gig economy, he walked each morning from his apartment to a traditional desk job. It was a good job, located in a high-rise skyscraper, that he'd been happy to line up before graduating from college in 2013, two years prior. But he couldn't stand it.

On a typical day, he finished his work within two or three hours. And then he spent the rest of the day desperately searching for something else—anything else—to do. His company wanted him present in the office but didn't provide enough work to fill the time.

At first, he proposed additional work projects. But it would take days for teams and supervisors to sign off on them, and even then, they'd usually be rejected. So he resorted to spending most of the hours between lunch and five o'clock reading every article on the tech forum Hacker News and watching Twitch, a website that broadcasts live feeds of other people playing video games. Less than two years into his professional career, Curtis was bored out of his mind and wasting a large part of his waking time.

One freezing January night, on his walk home, he decided he'd had enough of corporate employment. That night, he set his alarm for 6:45 a.m., three hours before his workday started.

When it buzzed the next morning, he carried his laptop computer to a nearby Starbucks, where he began working on a website he called "Crontent." The site would aggregate social media posts from Twitter, Facebook, and other networks into a single daily digest, so that a user could see all of the important news their friends had posted in one place. Its name was a play on the words "content" and "cron," the technical term for a programmed task that automatically repeats every day.

It was a terrible name. Most people who weren't programmers wouldn't get the joke. But that wasn't a problem, because Curtis didn't really plan for Crontent to have users. He hated selling, marketing, and advertising, which was part of what had made coding attractive in the first place. By building Crontent, he hoped to demonstrate to startups that he had serious skills.

After his morning Starbucks stop, he went to his day job. There, after finishing his work for the day, he scanned TechCrunch and Hacker News for startups that might have use for his abilities. This became his daily routine.

Weeks later, during this daily scan, a different kind of startup caught his eye. "Help build the world's engineering department," it advertised on its website.

He looked more closely. It seemed the site, called Gigster, wasn't looking for *employees* to help build the world's biggest engineering department. Instead, it wanted independent contractors, or "remote talent," who could work on their own schedules. "The nature of work is changing," the promo text read. "In the future, companies will leverage remote talent."[13]

While almost anyone could drive a car for Uber, Gigster had applied the gig economy strategy to software development, an area of expertise notoriously scarce. The Bureau of Labor Statistics projects that by 2020, there will be 1.4 million computer science jobs, but only 400,000 computer science graduates to fill them.[14] Which is why mere interns at companies like Facebook and Google make a higher wage than the average American worker.[15]

Gigster was successful partly because it was so expensive for companies to hire developers as full-time employees. It provided companies with a staff that they could pay per project, without worrying about building out elaborate perks like free meals and on-site dry cleaning that had become standard on tech company campuses.

Curtis had worked as "remote talent" once before, though he thought of the work as "freelance," which sounded less grand. During the summer before he left for university, he'd designed websites in his hometown on the eastern shore of Maryland. But that had been a way to make tuition money—he had never considered freelancing to be a career. He'd always imagined that he'd get a full-time job after college. Still, he was just bored enough to give Gigster a shot.

The only hurdle that might have stopped him was a long interview, the very thought of which made Curtis cringe. In college he had spent his free time on coding projects, like building scripts to formulate minute-song-snippet playlists for "power hours," a drinking game in which participants drink a shot of beer every minute for an hour. But he had a hard time focusing on subjects for which he could find no real-world applications, which included most of his classes and many of the questions tech companies asked during interviews.

When Curtis had interviewed at Google—which *Fortune* magazine named the best workplace for millennials in 2015— it had been a five-hour-long process. He had stood nervously in front of a whiteboard as various managers filtered into the room, asked him esoteric questions unrelated to the work he would actually do on the job, and watched him draw and explain his answers. He performed so poorly in his daylong interview that shortly after he had begun, he already knew he'd failed. It felt terrible.

Gigster's interview, he was relieved to find out, would follow a completely different process. It would be conducted via a typed chat. Rather than esoteric mind games designed to test theoretical knowledge, like the ones he'd completed while interviewing at other tech companies, all of Gigster's questions related directly to whether or not Curtis would be able to do the job. The company had no obvious reason to care if Curtis was a "culture fit," had growth potential, or worked well on a team. If he worked for Gigster, he would complete tasks alone. Only his current skills would matter.

Curtis answered questions like "If you had to implement [a particular piece of code], how would you do that?" "Ok, what if that didn't work?" This was the kind of problem solving at which Curtis thrived. He nailed the interview. Gigster invited only 7.7% of applicants to take gigs, and Curtis was one of them. Now he had to decide whether to take the non-job.

Though programmers on Gigster worked on projects for startups, freelance work didn't come with the same chance to hit it big that often lures people to early-stage companies. That chance belonged to employees who were paid partially in equity.[16] But joining Gigster did seem like a more interesting opportunity than sitting in a corporate office trying to pass the time.

Curtis wasn't one to quit his job immediately based on the promises of an unknown freelance service. Before he joined Gigster, he needed to do some due diligence. He'd already saved enough for a year's worth of expenses. Now he consulted an accountant. He researched health insurance plans and found that COBRA, a US program that would allow him to continue his current insurance plan, was too expensive. Purchasing the same plan that he'd enjoyed as an employee would, without his employer's contributions, cost him about $600 per month. Through the health exchange that had been set up as part of the Obama administration's Affordable Care Act, he found plans that would cost only $200 to $300 per month. On a spreadsheet, he laid out this cost, what he wanted to contribute monthly to his retirement savings account, and his expected taxes, which would double once he made the switch from employee to independent contractor. Then he browsed through Gigster's website, which listed available jobs and their compensation, to estimate how much he would need to work in order for Gigster to be viable.

At the end of the equation, he realized he could take home almost as much pay working as an independent contractor for Gigster as he did at his full-time job, around $10,000 each month. The gig economy struck him as a logical step between starting a company, which he wasn't ready to do, and working for the man, which he hated.

On a Friday in September, Curtis poked his head into his boss's office and told her that he was quitting to join the gig economy. His manager asked if there was anything that could make Curtis stay. There wasn't. The company gave him a choice about whether to work for two more weeks. Curtis decided he'd rather leave immediately. On his way out, he stopped at the company cafeteria and filled his backpack with free peanut butter bars, jalapeño chips, and a "shit-ton" of oatmeal packets. Liberal snack offerings had been the best part of his job.

The next day, a Saturday, Curtis ordered his usual Starbucks coffee and got to work.

He was free.

CHAPTER 3

THE BEST OF BAD OPTIONS

KRISTY MILLAND, A MOTHER OF ONE LIVING IN TORONTO, turned to the gig economy not out of a desire to become a millionaire or to leave her full-time job, but out of desperation.

While Kristy didn't have a college degree or access to capital, she did have a genuine entrepreneurial spirit: a willingness to try new things, to hustle, to start a business, and, when that didn't work, to start another business.

Many years ago, after dropping out of high school just before the birth of her daughter, she had worked to stretch a welfare check as her husband looked for jobs: She'd made spreadsheets showing which stores offered the best prices on every household item, repurposed leftovers, shopped with coupons, and bought baby clothes at the dollar store. Eventually she'd signed up for one of the first online education programs in Canada and finished her high school degree from home.

When her husband finally found a job at a temp agency, she taught herself how to build websites. She opened a daycare center. In addition to these ventures, she invented odd jobs like selling Winnie the Pooh Beanie Babies and Swarovski crystals—salvaged from garage sales—online. More unusually, she built fan websites for everything from kids' toys to television shows.

The most successful of these sites was a reality television fan forum she built from scratch. Kristy stayed up nights to watch live video feeds from the house where *Big Brother* was filmed (available online as part of the promotion for the show) and reported new developments among the house's residents before the edited episodes aired on television. To monetize the site, she taught herself how to sell ads and sold subscriptions.

Getting by became easier when a temp position Kristy's husband had landed at a Nestlé factory turned into a full-time job. (According to Kristy, he'd been making $11 per hour while, to his best knowledge, the temp agency collected around $17 per hour for his work.) Nothing changed about the work itself: The temp work was so similar to the full-time work that most managers didn't know which workers fell into which category. But his new hourly wage, nearly double what he'd made as a temp worker, combined with Kristy's odd-job entrepreneurship, allowed them to live more or less comfortably for 11 years.

And then, in 2007, the recession hit. Nestlé sold the factory where Kristy's husband worked, and Kristy knew she'd have to figure out finances all over again.

A survey commissioned by the Freelancers Union and Upwork in 2016 found that 20% of full-time freelancers in general don't have health insurance, compared to 10.3% of the non-elderly general population in the United States that went without insurance at the end of 2016.[1]

But in Canada, where Kristy and her family lived, losing her husband's health insurance wasn't quite as dire—healthcare was publicly funded. Kristy and her husband weren't going to miss out on seeing a doctor regularly because he'd lost his job. Still, prescriptions weren't fully covered, and they had ongoing health issues that, without his additional insurance, would cost them $250 per month (Canada's supplemental support for prescription drugs would only cover what they spent after the first $1,500).

Kristy's husband would be paid 11 months of severance—1 for each of the 11 years he had worked at Nestlé. But after that the family would need to have another source of income.

The *Big Brother* website did not make enough money to live on, and though Kristy was about to sell it for a modest sum (a wise move, considering that Twitter and Facebook were about to take over as platforms on which strangers discussed television shows), it wouldn't be the kind of sale that could support a family. Kristy had closed her daycare when she moved into a new neighborhood. And selling garage sale finds on eBay wasn't going to cut it.

In the few customer service jobs Kristy had taken at call centers years earlier, she had not enjoyed working under someone else's rules. Slowly, this preference for working at home had turned into a lack of experience working outside of the home. She hadn't waited on tables, had no experience in fast food, and had not learned any skills that might be particularly useful in a factory. She'd once applied for a job at McDonald's. Nobody had called her for an interview. Jobs were more difficult to find after the recession, and Kristy felt unqualified or too inexperienced for most of them.

But Kristy was someone who always figured it out. When I met her in 2015, she was in her late thirties, with long, blond hair that she sometimes wore tied in a scrunchie. She was not at all physically imposing—she owned a pair of baby pink crocs—but she had the sort of determination and strong belief in her ideas that would later inspire an academic researcher to describe her to me as intimidating. As a website moderator, she had picked fights with television channels that wanted to shut her down for spoiling show secrets. And as a daycare provider, when she'd been stiffed by most of her clients the week before Christmas (because they were also struggling to make ends meet), she had marched to each of their homes with a letter explaining that she could not afford her own Christmas dinner and demanding payment. If Kristy couldn't figure out how to make a living, it wouldn't be because she hadn't tried, and it wouldn't be because she wasn't a fighter.

Her first idea was to work more hours on Mechanical Turk.

Founded in 2005, Mechanical Turk is an online "crowdsourcing" marketplace run by Amazon. Its clients post work tasks on a dashboard that a "crowd" of workers can choose to complete. The process doesn't work that much differently than Gigster's process. But the tasks on Mechanical Turk are often simple and pay just cents each. They're jobs like adding tags to images, filling out spreadsheets with contact information, or writing product descriptions for websites. While programmers who sign up for gigs on Gigster are called "remote talent," workers who take small gigs on Mechanical Turk are called "crowd workers."

Because individual tasks on Mechanical Turk are often so simple and low paid, many assume that they're completed mostly by foreign workers who have a lower cost of living than people in the United States or Canada. But a UN International Labour Office report found that often crowd workers are more like Kristy. In the survey, which included workers on Mechanical Turk and a similar site called Crowdflower, 85% of respondents were Americans, 36.7% had a college degree, and 16.9% had a post-graduate degree. Almost 60% said they were unemployed before starting their gigs as crowd workers.

Kristy had started using Mechanical Turk when it launched in 2005 as a way to earn extra income in her downtime. She'd used the money to buy birthday presents and prizes for competitions she ran on her *Big Brother* forum. Now, in 2007, she would join the 28% of independent workers in the United States and 32% of independent workers in Europe who, according to the McKinsey Global Institute, have forgone the traditional job out of necessity rather than choice.[2]

To understand why Mechanical Turk exists, it helps to understand that the way technology "learns" is a bit like how a child learns. Teaching a young child to identify a cat by describing one isn't a great strategy. A cat has a tail and four legs. It has two small ears. But that could just as easily be a bear. If you really want a child to pick a cat out of a lineup, you need to find some cats and point them out. The child will start to build a mental blueprint for "cat," and eventually she'll recognize a cat when she sees one, even if it differs slightly from examples of "cat" that she's already experienced. It's more or less the same with machines. You could try to describe, say, a shoe, in a piece of code, but it's much more effective to say "Computer, here are 10,000 pictures of shoes. Now build a model for identifying a shoe."

One of Kristy's early Mechanical Turk jobs was to label thousands of pictures of garments and shoes with their colors. If presented with a photo of a blue shoe, she added a label that said "blue." If presented with a photo of a gray sweater, she added a label that said "gray." In this case, Mechanical Turk was Amazon's way of finding thousands of examples of each color so that it could train its algorithms to automatically sort searches for "blue shoes" and "gray sweaters." Improving technology in this way was one reason that Amazon had created Mechanical Turk.

Another reason was to compensate for technology's shortcomings with human intelligence. Amazon created one of its first applications that used Mechanical Turk in the days when people could email via cell phones, but couldn't yet access the internet. The idea was that people on their "mobile email" could send questions, such as "Where is the best restaurant near me?" and receive an answer almost immediately. It seemed like magic, but workers like Kristy were at the other end, Googling and answering for a penny per question.

Amazon had not launched the Mechanical Turk platform with a promise to create jobs, the way that Uber had early on bragged about adding "20,000 new driver jobs" to the economy every month. Rather, it had built the website as a way to integrate human intelligence with code—as a service for programmers. *TechCrunch*'s founder wrote shortly after the product launched that. "Amazon's new Mechanical Turk product is brilliant because it will help application developers overcome certain types of problems (resulting in the possibility for new kinds of applications) and somewhat scary because I can't get the Matrix-we-are-all-plugged-into-a-machine vision out of my head." He called the workers who would be doing the work "Volunteers."[3]

Early characterizations of Mechanical "Turkers" often portrayed them as people who were playing a game or passing the time while they watched television, which echoed the way that staffing agencies had portrayed temporary workers in the 1950s and 60s. As the UN International Labour Office report pointed out:

[The staffing industry] chose to promote the view that the work was done by middle-class housewives who were looking to earn "extra" money while still fulfilling their household duties. In 1958 the Executive Vice-President of Kelly Girl described "the typical 'Kelly Girl'" as someone who "[doesn't] want full-time work, but she's bored with strictly keeping house. Or maybe she just wants to take a job until she pays for a davenport or a new fur coat." Similarly, the temporary agency Manpower wrote in 1957 that temp work is "ideal for a married women with responsibilities that do not permit her absence from home every day of the week."[4]

This idea that early temp workers were just working for fun, to pass the time, or to buy frivolous items wasn't accurate. In a study of the temp industry from the early 1960s, 75% of women cited "to earn money" as the primary reason they worked, the majority saying they needed this money to meet daily needs. Decades later, in a tech-fueled era, the same portrayal wasn't quite accurate when it came to Mechanical Turk workers, either. In one survey, 35% of Mechanical Turk workers—not an insignificant portion—said they used the platform as their *primary* income.

Kristy hadn't ever attempted to make substantial income on Mechanical Turk before her husband lost his job. But she *had* found a forum for Mechanical Turk workers that would help her learn how to be more efficient while working on the site. In fact, she was already the lead administrator—which wasn't surprising to anyone who knew her well.

Since she had been a teenager, Kristy had gravitated toward pockets of online chatter. Her father had been one of the first computer engineers, and he'd introduced her to the internet while she was a high school student in the 90s. By today's standards, the early internet was comically slow. Kristy used a modem to dial into a local BBS (bulletin board system) and leave messages or take a turn in a game. The BBS only had one phone line—which meant only one person could be on the site at a time—and so she would log out and periodically check back to see if someone had responded.

Kristy had been a goth kid in high school—purple hair, piercings, black clothes—and she didn't have many friends in her class. But the forums she dialed into had local numbers, which meant that the people who she met online lived nearby. She liked them. They were all at least weird enough to seek out this odd new technology, and they were all at least smart enough to figure out how to use it. Kristy started attending GTs ("get-togethers") to meet members of her message boards offline. They played laser tag and paintball and went bowling together. It was her social scene.

Now the Mechanical Turk forum that she moderated, called Turker Nation, had a similar collaborative, friendly vibe. Workers, many of whom by this point she considered friends, shared tips and helped each other get the best work. Through them, she had found the short computer code that turned the Amazon product classification task—what color is this item?— from two clicks of the mouse (one to select a color, one to hit "submit") to a much faster single tap of the keyboard. She could hit the "y" key when an item was yellow, and the submission of the answer would be automatic.

A novice could not turn tasks like labeling images into a meaningful income. But with the help of the forum, it might be possible. And, Kristy figured, Mechanical Turk was available immediately, while looking for a job might have taken months. It didn't require her to have traditional experience, and it allowed her to make a living the way that she always had preferred—by figuring it out on her own at home.

Kristy started reading up on how to succeed on Mechanical Turk. In the meantime, she took two buses to a pharmacy across town where the filling fee was $4 instead of $14 and bought bigger-sized, cheaper pills that she cut down to the correct dosage with a knife. She stopped going to the dentist. When she noticed that the local Rib Festival was handing out samples of her husband's heartburn medication, she went back for the free medication the next day. And then the next three days after that.

When Terrence Davenport first heard the gig economy gospel of independence and flexibility in 2014, it sounded like the answer to his literal prayers.

Terrence had pretty much stopped praying after his mother died years earlier, but one morning, before he left for his volunteer job, he knelt down and asked God for help. What he was doing—working with kids in his hometown of Dumas, Arkansas, at a church free meal program—wasn't solving the bigger problems he saw in his community. He asked God to help him find a better way.

Dumas is a town of around 5,000 people in the Arkansas Delta that is surrounded by cotton fields once picked by slaves, then by sharecroppers, and, now, mostly by machines. Its residents on average make $22,000 per year, and almost 40% of the town lives in poverty.

Growing up, Terrence had never considered his family poor. Between the ages of five and ten, he'd lived with his mother and grandmother in an old sharecropper's house, which was part of his grandmother's compensation for working as a maid at the town's plantation. Later he'd moved into a house with his mother, where he lived on and off until graduating from high school. He had gone to bed every night with a roof over his head and never went hungry.

Not everyone he knew could say as much. Nobody in Dumas or Pine Bluff, where Terrence's father had lived, ever talked about their poverty, but Terrence remembered small moments throughout his childhood that gave it away. Like the time one of his friends noticed a slop bucket where Terrence's family scraped their plates after dinner—food for his uncle's hogs—and rescued a piece of pizza that was sitting on top of it. Food was food. And "poor" was a relative term.

Though Terrence didn't finish the chemical engineering degree he started at the University of Arkansas, he had taught himself how to code and how to design websites. Between the odd website job and his paycheck from selling shoes at a department store in Fayetteville, the city where he was living at the time, he was doing ok when he got the call that brought him back home.

His younger brother had fired a gun at a woman, who

sustained non-fatal injuries. He then had run away, and shortly later, he was discovered dead.

Terrence found the way the authorities had handled his brother's death to be suspicious. He had moved back to Dumas to take care of his grandmother, but also to investigate. As he pursued the question of what had happened that night, it opened other questions about what had happened to his community over decades. Why was the poverty rate among African Americans in Dumas more than double the poverty rate among white people in Dumas? In a county with as many African American people as white people, why were seven businesses in the county owned by African Americans, compared to 117 owned by white people?

Terrence had early on encountered racism. In high school, the white kids and African American kids had parked in separate parking lots. In college, a professor had failed him for turning in a paper that was too good, saying it couldn't be his work. Later, as a website designer, he'd lost a promising job as soon as he met the client in person. But this new line of questioning made him think about his community in a way that he hadn't considered before. It was one thing to not have access to opportunities that you were qualified for because of the color of your skin. It was another thing to not be qualified for the opportunities in the first place. Why were the people he'd grown up next to in Dumas so often hopeless, mistrustful, and seemingly unmotivated?

In order to fix the problems in Dumas, Terrence believed he had to study their origin. In records Terrence found at city hall and through interviews with elderly community members, he started piecing together a history of African Americans being cheated out of their land rights. And he started thinking about how the injustice of slavery, Jim Crow, and lynchings sparked trauma that could fester inside a family for generations. How these inherited wounds could compound to make people "unemployable."

Terrence's first attempt at helping his community was to join the church program that fed kids free meals. When only a few kids showed up, he started to ask kids in his neighborhood, "What did you eat today?" The question was meant to be specific, to address a problem in the way that simply asking "Are you hungry?" couldn't—because hunger, too, was a relative concept.

When it became clear that not everyone who needed a meal could get to the church on their own, he started a bus route of sorts, picking up kids in his Chevrolet Malibu to drive them to the meal program. On the ride, he tried to teach the kids how to think differently—to have hope and treat each other with more respect.

But he soon realized he couldn't teach kids without their parents' support, and that support didn't always come; in fact, some resented his efforts. It made some sense to him that parents took offense, for instance, when he told their children not to retaliate with violence if another child hit them. Their grandparents had been raised by people who remembered slavery, people who had been punished through violence and never had a choice about whether to fight back. So when Terrence said,

"Come talk to me instead of returning a punch," it could seem to these parents like he was teaching their children to be weak.

Lectures delivered during a 15-minute drive weren't enough to undo a deeply entrenched culture. Terrence decided he needed to find a way to reach parents. But how? What Terrence considered to be God's answer to this question arrived in a message from Dumas's superintendent of schools, who had once sat in on one of Terrence's Sunday school classes.

Terrence is a good teacher. He can tell the most heartbreaking story you've ever heard while still finding a moment to punctuate it with a blinding smile and a shot of optimism, and he has a way of breaking things into metaphors that makes them dramatic and understandable. Hearts are like fertile ground, he told me, while explaining why it was hard for the residents of Dumas to trust outside organizations. Experiences are like seeds.

The superintendent had been impressed when he'd dropped in on Terrence's class. Now he was trying to reach Terrence to tell him that a woman was in town to hire a teacher, and he wasn't going to let her leave until Terrence came for an interview. The message finally reached Terrence when the superintendent's niece found him at the food program.

Terrence didn't have enough time to study what the job entailed. He ran home, changed his shirt, and arrived in a sprint at the community technology center on Dumas's main street. The woman who met him there worked for a non-profit called Samasource that had, until recently, operated mostly in East Africa and India. Founded by a Silicon Valley social entrepreneur named Leila Janah, its mission was to "give work" to people living in extreme poverty. The idea was that giving a thing like food only temporarily met physical needs, but with work came dignity and a path out of poverty.

Since 2008, before Uber for everything, the non-profit had been making work contracts with tech companies like Getty Images, Google, and eBay. Those clients would have probably outsourced tasks such as tagging images or categorizing data in any case, but Samasource made sure they outsourced it to people living in extreme poverty. Now Leila Janah wanted to try a similar concept in the United States. Her organization had launched pilot programs in several California locations and now sought to expand eastward, to Dumas, Arkansas. The project was called "Samaschool."

At the interview, the woman told Terrence about how the gig economy might help end poverty in towns like Dumas, where great opportunities no longer existed and were unlikely to reappear. Workforce development typically involved attracting more businesses, or encouraging people to start new ones. Samaschool hoped the internet could help Dumas leapfrog this long, slow process. It would teach the town's residents how to access opportunity created elsewhere.

The Dumas program would work differently than the program that Samasource ran in other countries, where it hired workers to complete projects for US companies. Dumas workers would instead find their own opportunities through the gig economy.

Just a few hours after Terrence had prayed for a way to help his community, he felt as though he'd found it. "If I give you this dollar," he told me, "and then I put you on a deserted island, it's worthless." Work wasn't like that. Like land, it had inherent value. Terrence wanted the people in Dumas to unlock that value. He was definitely interested in the job.

The woman who interviewed Terrence told me she decided within moments of meeting him that he was the right fit for the project. He had charisma and energy, he had grown up in the area, and he was totally devoted to the cause of helping his community. Terrence came back to the tech center for another interview with Samaschool, and then another, the last one with its founder. He felt a connection with Leila, because they had the same passion. If he'd had the same network as Leila, the same access to resources, he imagined that he and Leila would have had a lot in common.

Why Dumas? he asked her.

Leila had run into the head of the Arkansas state economic development agency after speaking at the Clinton Global Initiative. He had opened the door for a pilot program in Dumas, which was funded by the Winthrop Rockefeller Foundation, a nonprofit focused on improving life in Arkansas. As Terrence remembers it, Leila talked mostly about the potential she saw in Arkansas.

To Terrence, it didn't really matter why Samaschool had come to Dumas. He was just glad that it was happening. And a couple of weeks later, when he got an email that let him know he'd been hired as a teacher, he was ecstatic to be a part of it.

He hoped that the gig economy—specifically Leila's vision for it—would play out in Dumas as it had been conceived in Silicon Valley, that it would serve as a conduit for opportunities that had otherwise left his small town, and others like it, behind.

CHAPTER 4

UBER FOR X

TRAVIS KALANICK JOINED HIS FIRST STARTUP MORE THAN ten years before co-founding Uber, dropping out of the University of California, Los Angeles, to work on a peer-to-peer music- and video-sharing startup. Airbnb's first founders met at the Rhode Island School of Design. Two of Upwork's cofounders created the freelancing site after working together, but from separate countries, on a previous startup.[1] Like most of the people who founded gig economy companies, these founders were experts in creating technology products, not in mobilizing and managing large service workforces. Most had little or no experience in the industries that they now set out to disrupt.

Among the horde of tech entrepreneurs who launched service-sector startups in the wake of Uber's funding announcement, Dan Teran and Saman Rahmanian made an unlikely pair.

Not only did they both depart sharply from the Mark Zuckerberg brand of young, nerdy founder, but they did so in nearly opposite directions.

Dan, with floppy blond hair, blue eyes, and the tall athletic build of a former college rugby player, could have looked like a preppy frat boy if he'd wanted. Instead, he went too long without a haircut, smoked openly, and developed a dry, sometimes biting, sense of humor. At 24, he could reasonably be described as cool.

Saman was in his early thirties, married, and a father of two—nearly a senior citizen by Silicon Valley standards. He didn't smoke, drink, or swear.

The two entrepreneurs met in 2013 at Prehype, a startup accelerator that partners with big brands to launch entrepreneurial ventures. Saman was a partner there and, along with the firm's other partners, interviewed Dan for a job.

Dan at that point didn't exactly have a stellar resume for an "entrepreneur in residence." For most of his life, he had wanted to be a politician: He'd organized a state Senate campaign for a former firefighter, received a college degree in a major he'd invented called "Urban Public Policy," and taken his first job out of college as a paralegal. His only experience with startups was his current job, as the first employee of a startup called Artsicle that sold art online.

But Dan had always been good at talking himself into things. His family joked that he'd talked his way into Johns Hopkins University (and in fact, his admission had involved tracking down everyone he could find who worked in the admissions department, many follow-up emails, and a promise— which he'd made good on—to be an extremely, extremely engaged student). When Dan had first decided that he wanted to work in tech, he started reading *TechCrunch* every day to absorb the culture and lingo—not an easy feat in the age of the buzzphrase "So Lo Mo" (in case you were not in the know circa 2011, this was short for "social, local, mobile" at a time when entrepreneurs were even less self-aware).

He'd landed the job at the "Netflix for art" startup partly because he knew a lot of artists. Or, at least, his roommate at the time was a photographer for the *New York Times*, and when he got invited to an interesting event, he brought Dan along to hold his flash. Dan had held a flash at an Alexander Wang fashion week party; at the Westway, a former strip club near New York's West Side Highway, as the fashion designer Valentino sang a karaoke version of "My Way"; and at the eightieth birthday party for Massimo Vignelli, a graphic designer known for creating the 1972 New York City subway map and other iconic designs. A few nights a week, he tagged along with his roommate to gallery openings. It was a reliable way to eat and drink for free.

As Artsicle's first employee, an experience Dan recounted in his Prehype interview, Dan had taught himself how to design a website, made art deliveries, and worked "like a dog." It was the best feeling in the world, knowing that a startup would succeed or fail based on your own efforts.

Saman liked Dan's hustle and "creative sensibility." He recommended him for the job. The project Prehype had thought Dan might work on fell through shortly later, but even though he wouldn't be paid until being assigned to another one (the Prehype partners worked on contract), Dan started showing up.

It was not exactly glamorous work. Prehype's office was

situated above a dumpling shop in New York City's China-town. Other tenants in the building included a garment factory and, according to the labels on boxes that regularly appeared in the freight elevator, a large importer of "fish balls." Under-neath a sign in the lobby that said "NO SMOKING, NO SPITTING, NO LOITERING," men often gathered to do all three.

Dan would sit in the small room that Prehype's six mem-bers shared and make calls for a project that Prehype was trying to land. He was essentially a volunteer.

Saman respected him for it. Showing up, whether or not there was work to do, had been a virtue drilled into him by his father, who had once worked as a government official in Iran and, for most of his childhood, had run a Persian rug busi-ness in Austria. Every day, at his father's insistence, the rug shop had opened exactly at 9 a.m. and closed exactly at 6 p.m. No matter what, it never opened a minute late, and it never closed a minute early—even if a customer hadn't been sighted all week. "Work is worship," Saman's parents used to tell him, in Farsi, referring to the Bahá'í belief that work should not be merely a means of earning money, but also an expression of service to humanity. It was because of this religion that the family had been forced to flee Iran, and Saman didn't take it for granted.

Eventually, Dan became a regular contractor on Prehype projects. When he and Saman worked together, they found they made a good team, bringing a complementary set of skills to assignments that involved building new products or launch-ing new services within large corporations. Saman was good with ideas. He enjoyed controlling every pixel in a product's design, creating a brand, and telling a story. Dan, meanwhile, was all about getting things done, even if it required 16-hour days and less-than-graceful maneuvering. And when it came to confronting a problem, he was nothing if not direct. When one of his neighbors, for instance, started throwing cigarette butts, used condoms, and other incriminating garbage onto Dan's porch, Dan collected a representative sample in a clear plastic bag and taped it to the neighbor's door. Efficient, effective, but perhaps not the most delicate personal branding effort.

More than one of Dan's friends described him to me as "salt of the earth." People he didn't like, who he generally did not pretend to like, had more colorful ways of describing his straight-talking manner. In either light, Dan was undeniably effective, and he soon developed a reputation for hard work and efficiency. By the time Saman had a startup idea that would change both his and Dan's lives, less than a year later, Dan had gone from an unpaid volunteer to partner.

Saman's idea for a startup was to offer a solution to the often shoddy practice of building maintenance, a problem to which Dan could relate, as his apartment had many issues beyond a teenager using his porch as a garbage can. He lived in the kind of Brooklyn apartment in which brown liquid could drip from the ceiling without causing much alarm (to the building's management, at least). The buzzer never worked, burnt-out hallway light bulbs remained in their sockets for months, and the front door was invariably broken. Sometimes the hot water tap ran cold. Other times, the shower temperature ran so hot it scalded his skin. He'd finally convinced building management to repair the dripping hole created by an upstairs neighbor's overflowing plumbing, but he had to spackle the drywall himself.

This housing situation was another aspect in which Dan differed from Saman, who lived in the kind of Brooklyn apartment building that included the name of its bathroom designer on the real estate listing. But even in a high-end apartment with floor-to-ceiling windows, bright white marble countertops, and multi-zone temperature control, Saman found managing his building's maintenance to be frustrating.

As Dan contemplated replacing hallway light bulbs himself, Saman—in an effort to make friends with the neighbors—had agreed to coordinate building maintenance for his condo board. He quickly regretted it. Keeping tabs on who had been in the building and what work they had done felt impossible. Why did it take a maintenance company six weeks to fix a broken lock? The superintendent was contractually obligated to sweep each week, but who could tell whether or not he had done so?

If Dan and Saman both had this problem, it was a vast one, which was one reason Saman wanted to solve it.

What he had in mind was a digital dashboard that could be posted in a building's lobby. Through it, building managers would be able to communicate with cleaning, maintenance, and other service companies and to track the work they'd done. Saman called it Managed by Q, after the character in James Bond movies who supplies all of the cool gadgets. He pitched the idea to Prehype's partners, and since he and Dan sat across from each other in a pod of desks, they ended up talking about it frequently. Dan started working on the project, too. Eventually, they decided that Dan should be a cofounder.

Saman's first target customers were condo boards like his own. He hired his building property manager to set up meetings throughout New York, and he and the company's first employee, a former real estate broker named Emma Schwartz (who had recently started an unrelated business selling ice cream made out of frozen bananas), took turns pitching Managed by Q at condo board meetings.

Saman had designed a logo—a white, bold Q on a black background—and mock product shots that made it look like Managed by Q and its technology were already well established. He, Dan, and Emma presented these on an iPad, along with stock photos of smiling people who had been photoshopped into black Managed by Q uniforms.

For $25 an hour, the entrepreneurs explained, condo boards could hire a cleaner or handyman through Managed by Q. More important, they would have access to an operating system for buildings. They could leave to-do lists, post notes for service providers, and track office supplies. Clients only had to pay for labor.

Selling to condo boards didn't work. Board members tolerated the pitch, but mostly wanted to wrap up the meetings so that they could have dinner with their families. As Dan put it: "Imagine pitching to people who don't give a shit and are just being nice to you." Only a small portion of the condo boards Managed by Q pitched actually said they would pay for the service.

If condos wouldn't buy it, maybe offices would. In late January, Managed by Q called every startup its founders knew and asked to speak to their office managers. Saman changed a few words in the pitch presentation. And within two weeks, about half of the 15 companies they'd pitched had purchased the service. Managed by Q, it turned out, was a service for offices—not condos.

All that existed of Managed by Q was a landing page that could handle credit card transactions and a pdf with app design ideas. The startup had promised its new clients that it would start cleaning their offices in April. Now it had just six weeks to both build the technology from scratch and figure out how to clean office buildings. Though the "future of work" would eventually become an important part of the Managed by Q story, Saman, Emma, and Dan didn't think about the gig economy or how work was evolving as they scrambled to launch the startup. They just needed to find cleaners—and quickly.

As engineers worked on the software, Emma, who at the time was in charge of operations, reached out to the companies that might provide office cleaners. The janitorial industry had been early to join the gig economy, though it didn't think of it that way. By the year 2000, 40% of janitors in the United States worked not for the companies whose offices they cleaned, but for janitorial companies, which typically charge clients a fee on top of their employees' wages.[2] Managed by Q, a contractor itself, would make the companies it partnered with contractors to contractors. That meant another layer of people taking a cut from the cleaners' work, and another layer between the people who owned the offices in which they worked and the people employing them.

Emma cold-called every cleaning company she could find in New York, offering an opportunity to work with what she assured them would soon be a hot new startup. Eventually two companies located in Long Island agreed to provide cleaners.

Managed by Q's founders sought to convey their company values to their newly subcontracted cleaners at a presentation on "how Q cleans." Of course, they weren't yet up to speed on the realities of squeegeeing windows and cleaning toilets. While they *had* mixed their own non-toxic cleaning supplies (Dan's brother was a chemist) and done some research about how to brand their service, the founders didn't have any real experience doing actual cleaning. Instead, they had an idea about how to make their service stand out.

The theory was inspired by the hotel industry. For the most part, it went, office workers, like hotel guests, only notice cleaners if something goes wrong: an un-emptied trash can, or an ominous-looking stain on their sheets. But hotels have figured out that they can create positive feelings among their guests by leaving noticeable signs that a room has been cleaned, like a turned-down bed or chocolates on a pillow. Managed by Q would do the same. The iPads Managed by Q planned to install on the wall of each customer's office would be one reminder that it existed. The startup would also leave branded

Managed by Q water bottles on every desk after the first cleaning and, in direct imitation of hotels, fold the end of every
toilet paper roll into a perfect triangle.

At an orientation session, Emma and Saman explained all
of this to their newly subcontracted cleaners, who had arranged
themselves around a big table in a borrowed conference room.
They demonstrated the Managed by Q iPad app, explaining
that their customers would be leaving feedback on the cleaner's work. "The office looks great!" read one example review
(in this hypothetical best-case scenario, none of the clients
used the feedback button to complain). Then Managed by Q's
founders took head shots of each of the cleaners, which would
be displayed on the iPad app, handed out black zip-up track
jackets and T-shirts—each branded with a white "Q" that
matched the water bottles—and hoped for the best.

In Silicon Valley, other "Uber for X" entrepreneurs were
solving the service portion of their businesses in a similar
way. Though some hired subcontractors, like Managed by Q,
and some hired independent contractors, like Uber, the mis-
conception behind both strategies was similar: "We'd build
this beautiful interface, and of course the cleaning just happens," Saman remembered thinking. "Of course the stuff just
gets done."

PART II

SUNSHINE, RAINBOWS, AND UNICORNS

CHAPTER 5

LIKE AN ATM
IN YOUR POCKET

THE PERCENTAGE OF ADULTS WHO EARNED SOME INCOME through websites like Uber, Airbnb, and Mechanical Turk grew 47-fold between 2012 and 2015, expanding to include around 4% of adults in the United States.[1] As the gig economy gained traction, Silicon Valley was sure that it would change the world. And it was equally sure, or at least seemed hell-bent on convincing itself, that the change would be wonderful.

This was typical of the tech industry, which tended to frame everything in terms of its world-changing positive social impact, sometimes to an unintentionally hilarious effect. ("Every day, in every way, the things that matter to our lives are coming to us," began one pitch for an on-demand fuel startup called WeFuel. "But there's something that still forces us to get in our car, fight traffic, and go through a ritual that is more than 100 years old. Filling up our cars with gas." The horror!)

Certainly most entrepreneurs in the gig economy didn't know much about the lives of low-wage workers, but the difference between getting attention from the tech press, which could help raise money, and remaining unknown was often a matter of telling the right story. This was before companies like Facebook came under scrutiny for their impact on mental health, privacy, elections, and housing prices in San Francisco, and grand pronouncements about tech as a driving force for good didn't feel as tone deaf as they might today.

Uber was, according to a 2014 press release along these lines, creating a powerful technology that "delivers turnkey entrepreneurship to drivers across the country and around the world." Explained Uber CEO Travis Kalanick: "For the first time, I think in possibly history, work is flexible to life and not the other way around."[2] He later stretched the talking point even further, suggesting on stage at the Global Entrepreneurship Summit that Uber itself was a social insurance of sorts. "In many ways, we look at Uber as the safety net for a city," he said, before asking the audience to imagine that a factory had closed down. What would happen to those workers? "They can push a button and get to work."[3]

This particular point became a go-to for gig economy entrepreneurs, who repeated themselves like pull-string toys that had been pre-programmed with only a handful of phrases.

"People are increasingly building flexible careers on their own terms, based on their passions, desired lifestyle and access to a much broader pool of opportunities than ever before in history," Stephane Kasriel, the CEO of Upwork, the largest freelance marketplace, commented in a 2015 press release.[4] Oisin Hanrahan, the CEO of Handy, a gig economy cleaning service, wrote in an editorial for *Wired* magazine that same year that "service providers have . . . signed up in droves because it provides income opportunities and flexible arrangements that may not have been available otherwise."[5] When I asked Stan Chia, Grubhub's COO, what the business case was for classifying the company's couriers as contractors, instead of answering the question, he said, "It affords the courier base the flexibility they want." Carole Woodhead, the CEO of Hermes UK, one of Britain's largest delivery companies, when responding to a claim that people only worked for the company because they were desperate, said that its workers "do not want to be employed," because they "like the flexibility . . . They like the ability to choose—the number of rounds they do, the number of hours they work."[6] No matter what the criticism or inquiry, if it involved the gig economy, you could reliably expect that the response would focus on flexibility.

These executives were right that the 9-to-5 job had become increasingly unrealistic for workers. Our collective idea that a "job" means working five days each week, every week, all year long came from a time when the ideal family included a male breadwinner and a female house worker. That setup was never really the case for a large percentage of American households, and it is even less common today, when more than 70% of mothers work for pay and women are the primary breadwinners in 40% of US households.[7]

The 9-to-5 job doesn't make much sense at a time when most families don't include a full-time, unpaid worker at home. It means that households often have to split three jobs—two out-of-home jobs and one at-home job—between two people, or, in the case of a single-parent household, one person has to take on two jobs. This puts an incredible amount of stress on workers (and especially women, who still shoulder a disproportionate amount of housework).[8] But instead of responding to this stressful situation with more flexibility or shorter hours, jobs have largely become more intense. A 1999 report from the UN International Labour Office detailed that the number of hours Americans worked rose throughout the 1990s. It concluded that they worked more hours than any other industrialized nation, including Japan, which has such a notorious overwork culture that the government has considered legally requiring workers to take five days of their vacation time every year.[9]

Outside of parenting, full-time jobs all but preclude the possibility of passion projects, volunteer work, or additional education, which is increasingly important as relevant skills evolve with technology. And, quite simply, people don't like their jobs. Annual Gallup polls between 2011 and 2015 have reported that around 70% of US workers say they are not engaged in their work.[10] The gig economy's flexibility was, from this perspective, undeniably appealing.

As the gig economy kicked off in 2013, it also looked like a potential solution for another pressing problem, which was that, even as many workers were struggling to juggle intense jobs with other responsibilities, a significant portion of the population was having trouble finding a job at all. Unemployment had fallen from its high of 10% in October 2009, but it still hovered at 6.6% in January 2014.[11] US inequality was the highest it had been since 1923.[12]

The press spent a lot of time covering how the gig economy might help, with their reactions to the idea that it could end unemployment ranging between "cautious but enthusiastic" to full-out, drink–the–Kool-Aid excited. *New York Times* columnist Thomas Friedman, among the latter camp, held that "these entrepreneurs are not the only answer for our economic woes . . . but they are surely part of the answer." A *Forbes* cover story in 2013 explained that the sharing economy and gig economy had created "an economic revolution that is quietly turning millions of people into part-time entrepreneurs."[13]

Tech journalists and bloggers, perhaps having spent too much time immersed in the optimism of entrepreneurs, typically went for full-out hype. "Will You Leave Your Job to Join the Sharing Economy?" prompted the tech blog *VentureBeat* in a 2013 headline.[14] The article's author had met a Lyft driver who also worked for TaskRabbit, a website on which neighbors could hire each other to complete odd jobs. She had also posted her apartment on the peer-to-peer lodging website Airbnb. "The combination of these three things is making her more money than she made working full time," the article's author gushed. "Plus, she feels like she's working for herself without the risk of starting her own company." The conclusion was in sync with Silicon Valley's vision: "I have a feeling 2013 is going to be a year where we start to hear about people leaving full-time employment to do a combination of different shared services so they can have a more flexible schedule."

It wasn't too far of a jump to extend this success story into a vision for the future of work, especially as on-demand apps launched for specific professionals like programmers, lawyers, interior designers, and even doctors.

"Uber, and more broadly the app-driven labor market it represents, is at the center of what could be a sea change in work, and in how people think about their jobs," *New York Times* columnist Farhad Manjoo wrote in January 2015. "You may not be contemplating becoming an Uber driver any time soon, but the Uberization of work may soon be coming to your chosen profession."[15] He continued: "Just as Uber is doing for taxis, new technologies have the potential to chop up a broad array of traditional jobs into discrete tasks that can be assigned to people just when they're needed, with wages set by a dynamic measurement of supply and demand, and every worker's performance constantly tracked, reviewed and subject to the sometimes harsh light of customer satisfaction."

Online freelancing itself wasn't exactly a revolution. Two of the first websites for hiring freelancers had been founded more than a decade prior, in 1999 and 2003. (Those websites had combined to form Upwork in 2013.) But the proliferation of "Uber for X" demonstrated how new technology could be used to manage workers as well as coordinate work among them. Even traditional websites like Upwork soon began mimicking the on-demand nature of these sites, with features that routed jobs to the right workers rather than asking employers to wait for responses to a job posting. "We're trying to move toward an on-demand model," Shane Kinder, Upwork's vice president of product, told me in an interview. "We'd love to be in the world where we enter information and instantly get back a freelancer who is qualified to do the job and is ready to do it now."

Startups that offered specific types of work, like Gigster, had already set that dynamic up, often by thoroughly screening the freelancers they worked with in advance. One company, called Konsus, offered a "full e-commerce experience" for such business services as creating PowerPoint presentations. Its clients could purchase graphic design work for $29 per hour, or research work for $35 per hour, by clicking "get started now." Konsus then found an appropriate freelancer and delivered the project.

Academia stretched the concept of on-demand workers even further. A researcher at Stanford who studies "gig work" built a computer program that automatically managed complex projects.[16] When one step was completed, the system automatically hired a freelancer for the next step, on-boarded him or her, and handed off the project. One of the trial teams successfully turned napkin sketches for new apps into functional prototypes—and recruited users to test them—all within a single day.

Another group of researchers at a nonprofit research center called the Institute for the Future created a project called "iCEO" that similarly automated the coordination of freelance work. For one task, they programmed the software to prepare a 124-page research report for a Fortune 50 company. By automatically coordinating work by writers, editors, proofreaders, and fact-checkers on various online platforms, it completed the report, which would have usually taken weeks, in three days.[17] The researchers didn't even really have to manage the project. Quality checks and HR processes were also freelance assignments. In one meta-example, a contractor hired through a website called oDesk completed the task "hire oDesk contractors."

It was becoming easier and easier to imagine a point at which any type of work—no matter how complicated or how dependent on the work of a team—could be ordered with the click of an app. The 9-to-5 job, as a concept, could disappear altogether.

Gig economy startup valuations soared as quickly as these expectations. In the six months between June and December 2014, Uber more than doubled its paper value to investors, jumping from a $17 billion valuation (an amount the *New York Times* called "eye-popping"[18]) to a $40 billion valuation.[19] It was only a matter of time before the gig economy was expected to create more "unicorns," the tech world's nickname for startups with valuations higher than $1 billion.

Though it was still early days for the majority of gig economy companies, some had passed promising milestones. Postmates, a courier delivery service, had by 2014 expanded from a one-person startup to a more than 20-city operation, and it would soon win partnerships with giant, established brands like Starbucks and McDonald's. Grocery delivery company Instacart in 2014 said it was on track to generate $100 million in revenue, ten times the amount it had earned during the previous year. Handy expanded to 28 cities and signed up 5,000 cleaners. When the company passed $1 million in revenue in a single week, *TechCrunch* turned the milestone into a story: "Our cleaners say," Handy's CEO told the blog, that "it's like an ATM machine in your pocket."[20]

CHAPTER 6

UBER FREEDOM

AFTER QUITTING HIS PROGRAMMING JOB TO BECOME A full-time freelancer with Gigster, Curtis no longer stuck to his early morning routine of taking his laptop to Starbucks. Seeking variety, he had scoped out all of the cafes near his apartment that had dependable WiFi. Sometimes he worked at the library. At others, he might work at the park or a bar. On his own schedule, he roamed between these places, and he was happy doing it. Two months into his freelancing career, Curtis was earning as much as he had in his full-time job: between $10,000 and $12,000 every month. He also now had time to hit the gym in the middle of the day, meet his girlfriend on her lunch break, and plan multiple vacations. For him, Silicon Valley's utopic description of the gig economy seemed completely true.

At his 9-to-5 job, Curtis had hated everything except his data-mining work: the office politics, the long chains of command, and the "selling" and self-promotion required to advance in the organization or do something new. But on Gigster, there was none of that. If he took on projects and did them well, his ranking, what the platform called his "Karma" score—based on how many projects he successfully completed—increased. And as his score got stronger, Gigster's algorithm "trusted" him with more and more interesting projects. It was advancement without all of the extra stuff required to succeed in a traditional career.

Almost every gig economy company had created a similar rating system. Uber asked riders to score drivers on a five-star scale after every ride (drivers did the same for riders). Handy, the gig economy cleaning company, used the same scale. Upwork allowed customers to leave workers comments and star ratings that showed on their profiles. Because gig economy companies didn't have managers who knew workers, they relied on these ratings to algorithmically dole out rewards and punishment, such as "deactivation," the gig economy term for getting fired (e.g., removed from the platform). Rating systems like these could replicate prejudice or feel arbitrary to some workers, but Gigster's system worked for Curtis. Not only was he able to land enough jobs to make a living, but they were increasingly interesting. Sometimes he learned new skills in the process of completing them.

Of course, there were some downsides to Curtis's new gig economy lifestyle. He had to work every hour that he got paid. There were no more paid hours spent watching video game sites, and no more free snacks. When he got called for jury duty in March, he lost a week of income. Though there's no federal law that requires employers to offer paid leave for jury duty (some state laws do), more than 60% of US workers, and 81% of US professionals and managers, collect a paycheck while they serve.[1] As an independent contractor, Curtis didn't have that luxury.

But these downsides were manageable. Curtis had a year's worth of savings that, because he had made money every month through Gigster, he had not even touched, and so jury duty didn't threaten his ability to buy groceries. It meant he'd spend the next month catching up on projects. The loss of free snacks and a guaranteed paycheck were far outweighed by the freedom and challenging work that accompanied his new gig.

By April, seven months into his freelance career, Curtis no longer wanted a job at a startup. "I don't see what it can offer me that is better than my current situation," he told me. "The risk [with joining a startup] I think is actually greater than freelancing, because startups pay you less, and equity is pretty much worth nothing." I reminded him of rare cases like Uber, in which a startup becomes worth tens of billions of dollars, making early employees with equity instant millionaires. But Curtis preferred to focus on his regular paychecks rather than the odd chance of a huge payout. Freelancing suited him.

This was the gig economy that its boosters described, and Curtis proved that it could indeed work out wonderfully.

The same personality traits that made Abe a competent server—a loud, faux confidence and a natural ease with strangers—also worked well for him as an Uber driver. When he was driving for Uber, he played "old-school" music, always offered gum, and sometimes offered shots of whiskey. "Pretty much whatever they wanted to do, I was up for it," he said. "Like, they wanted to drink in the backseat, that's fine by me. Just don't make a mess. Whatever." Videos Abe posted on social media showed passengers dancing in the backseat, Abe's head bopping to the beat as he gripped the steering wheel. He called this "the Uber difference."

Uber doesn't allow riders to request specific drivers, but Abe created a system with his best passengers that he called "shot-gunning a ride." Instead of requesting a ride in the app, these clients would first call Abe directly. After entering his car, they'd open the app and request a ride. Since Abe was the closest driver in this scenario, Uber would almost always route the request to him.

Abe mostly drove at night, and he usually started near the same row of popular clubs and bars where his friend had first shown him how to work on the Uber app. His customers were often drunk, "Which I actually prefer," he said, "because they are easy to get along with." Apparently the feeling was mutual: According to emails he showed me, Abe scored a 4.9 rating on Uber's five-star system.

Uber offered him the same deal that it had offered the friend who signed him up. If he referred a driver to the platform, he'd earn a $200 bonus after that driver's twentieth ride (Uber made variations of this deal in different cities and during different time periods). Abe had plenty of experience getting people to sign up for things, though most of it was related to what he eventually learned were pyramid schemes. Convincing people to drive for Uber, a company that would actually pay them, couldn't be more difficult than getting them to join GIN. In April 2015, Abe made a Facebook page called "Uber Freedom" ("because it's Uber, and it gives you freedom") and started posting about the thrills of being an Uber driver. His hope was that others would sign up using his referral code, which he would promote through the same Facebook page.

His first video showed a large blond dog in the back of Abe's Nissan Altima. "This is Waylon, my newest Uber rider," Abe says as he films with his phone. "I'm going to give you five stars, Waylon."

True to the "law of attraction" that he'd learned through GIN, Abe was absolutely sure other people on Facebook would want to imitate this new Uber lifestyle he'd chosen.

Two years had passed since Kristy's husband lost his job at the Nestlé factory. Though he'd gone back to school to finish his high school education, he still hadn't been able to find a job. Kristy meanwhile had become highly proficient at making money on Mechanical Turk: In both 2011 and 2012, she earned more than $40,000 on the platform. That was before taxes, but it was still an astounding amount relative to other Mechanical Turk workers.

According to a 2016 report from the UN International Labour Office, "crowd workers" like Kristy, 40% of whom rely on crowd work as their main source of income, on average earn between $1 and $5.50 per hour.[2] The median hourly earnings of Mechanical Turk workers based in the United

States is $4.65 per hour, while for Mechanical Turk workers based in India, it is $1.65 per hour. Based on a 40-hour work-week (which she often exceeded), Kristy was earning more like $20 per hour. She had achieved this relatively high rate by learning how to find the best jobs and how to set up systems that made them easier to complete.

Beginners on Mechanical Turk were pretty much useless, because they didn't qualify for higher-paying tasks that required a certain amount of past work to access, tended not to apply any strategy to the tasks they chose, and didn't always understand how to complete them efficiently. I knew because I was one. Curious to understand how Mechanical Turk worked, I logged on one day and tried the work myself.

The site has none of the polish of Amazon's other products. It looks old, like an internet forum from the early 2000s, which perhaps suggests its low placement on Amazon's list of priorities. Human Intelligence Tasks (HITs), as they're called, appear in a dashboard. You can sort them to find those available for your "qualifications," which can include attributes such as being based in a certain country or having successfully completed a certain number of tasks. When you choose a HIT, based on a short description like "transcribe 35 seconds of media into text," you complete it inside of the platform and earn a sum every time you hit "submit."

It only took me five minutes to set up an account and just a few minutes after that to locate tasks for which I qualified. But it took me almost an hour to make a dollar. Most of the tasks I selected involved taking surveys for academic studies or labeling things. The task I spent the most time on was one posted by a Microsoft researcher who was building image recognition software and needed to "teach" the algorithm how to spot and name objects. One by one, I labeled a series of hundreds of animal pictures. Each slideshow had five photos of the same type of animal in a different type of scene. Each photo in these slideshows had 11 pages of labels, which meant that one slideshow took 55 clicks to complete. I got paid $0.05 every time I completed a slideshow.

After a few rounds, I found myself hoping for bird slideshows. Birds were usually outside and alone when photographed, which meant that most of the labels in my arsenal—bed, person, window, table, ball—did not apply. I only needed to click and drag one label: bird. A dog in a car's passenger window, on the other hand, required the labels "car," "mirror," "dog," and "person." If that person happened to be on the phone, it also required "cell phone," and if there was traffic on the street, it might require "motorcycle." Birds, by requiring just one label, saved me valuable seconds, and my wrist valuable exertion, as I flipped through the slideshows. After two hours—the time it took before I got dizzy and moved on—I had completed 61 slideshows and made $1.94 per hour. From this perspective, Kristy's $40,000 earnings seemed incredible.

Some of her more remunerative work came from employers who posted hundreds or thousands of tasks at a time that could be completed in rapid succession. Kristy would install small software programs that allowed her to complete, say, a simple categorization task by hitting a key on her keyboard ("y" for yellow or "b" for bird) rather than clicking a mouse. Categorizing an item every five seconds for an hour at $0.03 per image would pay $10.80 per hour. She also took on more complicated tasks that paid better. Writing descriptions for product sites, for instance, could pay $1.50 per paragraph. So if she did one every five minutes, she would make $18 an hour. It was a matter of doing the work quickly and sticking with it for a long time.

Turker Nation had a forum where workers alerted each other about these "good work" opportunities, which paid well and could be completed in large batches. To make sure that she didn't miss any of them, Kristy set up an automated system that, when a new "good work" task was posted, would check to see how much it paid and whether she met its qualifications. If she was eligible for a task that paid $0.05, her computer would alert her with a "ping" noise. If she was eligible for a task that paid between $0.05 and $0.25, her computer would sound an alarm that sounded like a laundry machine finishing. If she was eligible for a task that paid more than $0.25, a siren would sound.

No matter where Kristy was in her house, if she heard the alarm go off, she would run to her computer. There were thousands of other Mechanical Turk workers who were competing with each other to grab the high-paying work, which was assigned to whoever could claim it first. Kristy would sleep in her office so that she could listen for the alarm to go off at night without waking her husband up. When she spotted good tasks, often through her alarm system, she used an automated tool to keep her queue full with the maximum 25 tasks that could be assigned to her at one time, and then worked furiously to finish them and grab more before they were snatched by other people.

One of the tasks she didn't like to miss was answering questions from Amazon's Q&A service. These were posted every 15 minutes, and there were two aspects that made them good tasks. The first was that people often asked the same questions, and Kristy had compiled a spreadsheet of answers that made these common questions quick to answer. She could get through a batch of several hundred in about five minutes. The second was that, to incentivize good work, each month Amazon paid a bonus of a few hundred dollars to the worker whose answers received the highest number of "thumbs up" votes from users. Each question might only pay a penny, but this bonus was significant. It meant that Kristy never wanted to miss a batch. Her routine was to listen for the alarm, complete the batch in five minutes, take ten minutes off, and then get back to work when the next batch of questions dropped.

Another Amazon task that she prioritized was one that allowed customers to take photos of products in stores in order to find the same product on Amazon. It was how the company encouraged customers to comparison shop, but not everyone used this feature of Amazon's app as intended. When they sent pictures of genitals, Kristy sent back a link to a book called *I'm Calling the Police* (the system was set up so that she could only communicate through links to Amazon products). It was worth dealing with rude inquiries like these because she had found a way to earn extra money when Amazon's users sent photos of actual products: She sent them her affiliate marketing links and earned a percentage of purchases they made after clicking on them.

Kristy also started proactively asking clients if they needed help designing their requests, contacting them through the Mechanical Turk site. Sometimes she collected consulting fees for her advice.

The paradigm on both the employer and worker side of Mechanical Turk was less of a relationship between two colleagues than it was two people trying to beat a system. In one common example, companies posted the same work three different times on Mechanical Turk in order to check its accuracy. If one worker submitted a different answer than the other two who completed the task, the company assumed that worker had given a bad answer and rejected her work (which meant she wouldn't be paid for it). To beat this system on the worker side, all a Mechanical Turk worker needed were two accounts to agree with each other. Some Turkers built automated bots to submit arbitrary (but matching) work results. The bots collected payment because they agreed, while a person who had earnestly done the work didn't get paid. All Turkers could do when someone rigged a task this way was to tell each other to avoid it.

Kristy didn't feel like she could leave her apartment, or even her computer, lest she miss out on an opportunity to work on good tasks. Unlike an employee at a fast-food restaurant or a cleaning company, she didn't get paid for any downtime, and

she could earn more money by working smarter and faster. The
psychology was that of a game that required her to be constantly on alert. In a way, that psychology kept her going: She'd
set a goal for $100 per day, and, cent by cent, she often met it.

In Dumas, Arkansas, Terrence busily recruited students for the
class that would teach them how to succeed in the gig economy. To advertise the new Samaschool program, he took out
an ad in the Dumas *Clarion*, the local newspaper. It used the
same language as Silicon Valley: His class would turn students
into internet entrepreneurs who worked for themselves.

Among the 30 students who passed Terrence's initial interview were farmworkers, home care workers, and a few people
who were chronically unemployed. Even a local elementary
school teacher showed up. Samaschool's plan was to teach students how to use the digital freelancing website Upwork (then
two sites called oDesk and Elance), one of the biggest digital
freelancing websites, to find work. Jobs in research, data en-
try, or customer service—all of which were plentiful on
Upwork—didn't require college degrees. All Dumas's residents needed to obtain the work, the thinking went, was some
instruction on how to promote themselves effectively and an
internet connection.

Terrence held the classes in the same community technology center where he had sprinted to his job interview. Built in
2012, the tan brick building had the look of a miniature high
school. It was equipped with a pod of public computers, a work-

force development office, and two large, bright classrooms in which local universities offered courses. Samaschool's classes took place in the same classrooms, each outfitted with long rows of white desks topped with black PCs.

As students searched for jobs in the gig economy, they weren't always successful. But Terrence started searching on their behalf, and slowly but surely, a handful of students began working online, in a way that they hadn't previously imagined was possible.

A year after Terrence got started, I visited Gary Foster, one of his most successful students. Gary lived at the time in a neat trailer nested so close to the railroad tracks that it literally shook when a train passed. The door was open, and the doorbell was broken. "Hello?" I yelled into the screen.

"Come in!" I heard from somewhere inside.

I found Gary in a small square room filled with Tweety Bird stuffed animals—his wife's favorite. He was sitting at a table behind two laptop computers lined up side by side. We shook hands as he pulled on a headset. It was only after we heard a high-pitched "ding!" that I understood why he hadn't answered the door.

"Hello and thank you for calling Sears home warranty," he said in a calm, confident voice. "My name is Gary, how can I help you?" He then dove into a conversation about a broken air conditioner with a man who lived in New York City, pulling up reference materials and customer service scripts on his computer as he spoke.

Until recently, Gary had worked at a local dog food

plant, but he'd been laid off when the plant was sold to a new company. He'd heard about Terrence's class when he was at the workforce center, applying for jobs. For a few months after losing his job, Gary had worked the night shift at a Tyson plant about an hour away from his home. But he hated the long, nighttime commute, which scared him. "At any moment, anything can run in front of your vehicle and tear it up," he said. "You break down in the road out here, and you're stuck until someone comes to get you.

"Down here," he reiterated, "there ain't no jumping on the bus."

Gary didn't get any jobs through Upwork. But Terrence had found him placement at a huge customer service company called Arise. Nine of Terrence's students qualified for similar jobs, but only three, Gary included, had internet access fast enough to meet the companies' specifications.

Gary wouldn't be directly employed by Arise. He wouldn't even be directly contracted to work. Arise hires subcontractors it calls "independent business operators" (IBOs), who in turn hire the people who actually answer phones. Terrence had found an IBO that was looking for new independent contractors.

On the website of Gary's new employer, under a slideshow of white women in headsets with too much makeup and photoshopped white teeth, an application page explained why this employer was superior to others like it: "We offer above minimum wage with pay increases," one bullet point said, "when others offer [pay] by the minute." Offering more than the minimum wage, it seemed, had become something to brag about. After all, the law does not require companies to ensure that independent contractors make more than a minimum wage.

Imagine a nesting doll with Gary at the center: Gary was the smallest doll, an independent contractor working for the IBO (the company with the bullet points and smiley slideshow). Go one layer bigger, and you'd see the IBO (the small business that hired Gary). Another layer bigger, and you'd see Arise, the big customer service company that had made a contract with the IBO. Only after another layer would you find Sears, the company that the customer thought he was dealing with all along.

Arise, no surprise, presented this setup as innovation: Under the heading "Leveraging the power of crowdsourcing," the company's "about" page at the time explained to potential customers that Arise takes advantage of "innovative breakthroughs in technology and our own award winning, proprietary and patented technologies" and "provide[s] entrepreneurial opportunities to many underserved populations, where small business owners have the ability to create flexible schedules based on their lifestyle needs." Silicon Valley hadn't been exactly original in the way it had pitched its services as world-changing innovation. Companies like Arise were the predecessors to the gig economy.

Thanks to Terrence's negotiations, Gary did not have to pay for his training, which some in his position did. But he also did not get paid for the three-week, four-hour-per-day program.

And during that time, he had trouble paying his bills. "I had disconnection notices everywhere," he said. In July, he'd received an official offer for (not quite) employment that seemed to contradict itself: "This is At-Will Employment and you are being paid as a contractor. You will be responsible for any and all applicable taxes due to State and Federal agencies." Appended, a hiccup of seemingly self-contradicting good cheer: "Welcome to the company." His pay would start at $9 per hour, $1.50 above Arkansas minimum wage at the time.

Gary, a father of eight (one of whom lives with him) and a grandfather of eleven (with the twelth on the way, the last time I talked with him), was good at customer service. Workers like him were measured on three standard industry metrics: schedule adherence (whether they worked the amount of time they had agreed to work), average hold time, and call quality. He told me he usually scored in the top 5% on all three.[3]

"My voice is pretty straightforward, pretty calm," he said. One time, he took a call from someone who was so angry that he threatened to place a claim for every outlet, every light, and every ceiling fan in his house, and for ten toilets.

Gary let him vent. Finally, the man admitted, "You know I don't have ten toilets."

"I'm pulling up the claims, but I'm not putting them in," Gary told him. "I was waiting for you to calm down."

Once he completed his training and started to work, Gary's life appeared to be on the upswing. With his new paycheck and his new flexibility, he was planning a trip to Hawaii to celebrate his fifteenth anniversary with his wife. "We never went on a honeymoon," he said, smiling already at the thought of his beach vacation. He was trying hard at his non-job, and it was working for him—at least for the time being.

Gary, like Kristy and others who turned to the gig economy out of necessity, may have chosen it based on limited alternatives. But like Curtis, who had been drawn to the gig economy lifestyle, or Abe, who had been drawn to the opportunity to be an entrepreneur, he started out full of hope.

PART III

FINE PRINT

CHAPTER 7

A COMPETING STORY

AS THE GIG ECONOMY AGED, IT BECAME CLEAR THAT independence, flexibility, and freedom were not its only characteristics—that the experience wasn't wonderful for everyone.

One of the most startling reports was *Washington Post* reporter Lydia Depillis's September 2014 profile of an independent cleaner named Anthony Walker. In it, Walker dropped his four-year-old daughter off at daycare and dragged a roller bag full of cleaning supplies onto a Washington, DC, city bus, which he rode for more than two hours before reaching the home he'd been assigned to clean. The job, assigned to him by the gig economy company Homejoy, paid $51, which meant that, including five hours of commute time, Walker made around $10 per hour—before any taxes had been withheld and without any workers' compensation, unemployment, time off, or retirement benefits. This was better than nothing, perhaps, but it didn't look much like the story that Silicon Valley had been telling about the gig economy.[1]

Throughout 2014 and 2015, stories like these made it hard to accept the idealistic idea that the gig economy would provide quality on-demand work in an economy in which good jobs were becoming harder to find. There were reports of drivers who had been deactivated from Uber without explanation. Cleaners for Homejoy who didn't earn enough to pay rent. And couriers who worked for gig economy delivery companies like Postmates and Deliveroo who didn't clear the minimum wage.

"I think Deliveroo wants to manufacture this image that we are all young, middle-class men who wear trendy clothes, making a little extra cash," one courier told *The Guardian*. "But a lot of the couriers are migrants, or working-class people from the local area, and the majority are doing it full-time because they need the money." (Deliveroo told the paper that 85% of its fleet used the gig as supplemental income.)[2]

Workers in the gig economy were disproportionately poor. Compared with the American population, about twice as many gig economy workers earned less than $30,000 per year,[3] below what MIT calculates to be the US living wage for a family of four. In New York City, where the living wage for a family of four is $46,000 in a year, a group that said it represents 50,000 ride-hail drivers told the *New York Times* that more than one-fifth of its members earned less than $30,000 in a year, before expenses.[4] When gig economy leaders had conveyed their visions early on, they had failed to distinguish between the experiences of people with relatively scarce skills—freelance graphic designers, journalists, movie production crews, programmers—and those with less scarce skills, like house cleaners and drivers and Mechanical Turk workers.

As a group, independent contractors earn more than employees who do similar work. Many of them are highly skilled freelancers like Curtis, the New York City–based programmer, and make six-figure salaries or more.[5] But low-wage workers have historically been hurt rather than helped by the trend away from employees. One study found that contracted cleaners and security guards earned 15% less and 17% less, respectively, than their in-house peers.[6] Another study found that the "outsourcing wage penalty" ranges between 4% and 7% for janitors and between 8% and 24% for guards. Both groups were less likely to receive benefits than their counterparts with direct-employment ties to their work.[7]

A report published by the US Government and Accountability office in 2015 found that contingent workers across the board—a category that includes temp workers and subcontracted workers in addition to freelancers—earned about 10.6% less per hour than "standard workers," and were about two-thirds less likely to have a work-provided retirement savings plan. "These contingent workers are also more likely than standard workers to experience job instability, and to be less satisfied with their benefits and employment arrangements than standard full-time workers," wrote the report's authors. "Because contingent work can be unstable, or may afford fewer worker protections depending on a worker's particular employment arrangement, it tends to lead to lower

earnings, fewer benefits, and a greater reliance on public assistance than standard work."[8]

The economist David Weil argues in his book *The Fissured
Workplace* that there are several reasons workers' pay and benefits are stronger when workers are permanent employees at a
larger company than when they work as independent contractors, for a contractor, or for a temp agency. He writes:

Large firms employing a wide spectrum of workers—
from highly trained engineers and professional managers, to semiskilled production workers, to janitors and
groundskeepers—characterized the workplace of the
mid-twentieth century. An important consequence of
having people with diverse skills and occupations working under one roof was that companies shared the gains
received from their market position with the workforce.
They did so through how wages were set—in both union
and nonunion workplaces. While some businesses shared
gains out of corporate beneficence, many did so because
of what might be called enlightened self-interest. Because
feelings about fairness affect employee morale, fairness
considerations have an impact on human resource policies, including wage determination. In particular, per-
ceptions about what one is paid depend in part on
what others are paid. If a large company employed executives, secretaries, engineers, mechanics, and janitors, it therefore needed to be cognizant of how the
structure of wages was perceived among all those

working underneath the common corporate umbrella. As a result, janitors' wages were pulled up because of the wages lead employers paid their factory workers.[9]

When companies instead look to contract a janitor, Weil writes, it is no longer a question of "What is fair?" but rather a question of "Which company is offering the best price?" Meanwhile, offering an independent contractor access to the company healthcare plan becomes a legal liability (because it may be used as evidence that the worker is misclassified) rather than a legal imperative.[10]

You can see a stark divide between employees and non-employees on the campuses of rich technology companies like Facebook, where the highly paid knowledge employees have access to free perks, but the contracted cleaners, bus drivers, and security guards do not. "They have free laundry, haircuts, free food at any time, free gym, all the regular things that you have to pay for, but they have it for free," Maria Gonzalez, a janitor at the company, told *The Guardian* in 2017. "It's not the same for janitors. We just leave with the check."[11]

Facebook at least pays its contractors well, having set a $15 minimum wage. But other companies flat-out abuse their non-employee workers.

Temporary workers have a higher rate of injury than traditional employees, reporting incidents between 36% and 72% more often than non-temporary workers.[12] One of the more drastic examples of abuse against other forms of contingent workers demonstrates how large companies can escape responsibility for the safety and fair treatment of workers they don't directly employ: A *USA Today* investigation in 2017 revealed that port truck drivers in Los Angeles often owed money to their employers at the end of the week despite working 20 hours per day. Companies took workers' pay and put it toward the ownership of their trucks, but took their trucks without returning any pay if the workers failed to please (which in one case merely involved missing a day of work).[13]

Los Angeles port truck drivers are part of a delivery system that moves products to big retail chains. In every case, the response to these allegations by companies that depended on these workers (but hadn't technically employed them) was the same. When the *USA Today* reporter asked a Target spokesperson about labor violations by trucking companies in Target's supply chain, the Target employee wrote that "Target doesn't have anything to share here." A JCPenney spokesperson told him the company "relies on its third-party transportation vendors to comply with all applicable laws and regulations." A spokesman for LG Electronics said that "We're not trying to wash our hands of this issue, but it's frankly far afield" and "really very disconnected from LG Electronics."

Similarly, when the National Employment Law Project (NELP) sued grocery stores in Manhattan on behalf of workers, one of whom had worked 10- to 12-hour days, seven days each week, for a weekly salary of around $90, NELP reported to a US Senate Committee, "The stores said the workers were not their employees, and the labor brokers said the deliverymen were independent contractors."[14]

• • •

Gig economy champions are fond of touting data that shows that workers like flexibility. But this data doesn't take into consideration how much workers value this flexibility when weighed against factors like pay, job security, benefits, and safety. The National Bureau of Economic Research devised a study to try to understand how workers actually value flexibility, as opposed to whether they think it's a good idea. Princeton economist Alexandre Mas and Harvard economist Amanda Pallais recruited call center workers and asked more than 3,000 job applicants to choose between a job that offered a standard 9-to-5 schedule and the same job, but with one of five flexible scheduling options. They randomly varied the difference in pay between the two jobs. Sometimes the jobs paid the same. Sometimes the alternative work arrangement paid more, or a lot more, than the traditional job, and sometimes the traditional job paid better.

Mas and Pallais found that when workers chose between the two types of jobs presented to them—one an alternative work arrangement and one a traditional, office-based 9-to-5 job—workers overwhelmingly placed little actual value on flexible options. When the traditional and flexible scheduling options paid the same, for instance, only a slight majority—60% of applicants—chose the option to schedule their own hours. On average, they were willing to take a $0.48-per-hour pay cut to set their own schedules, but they weren't willing to give up any pay at all to set their own number of hours. In other words, they placed some value, but not a huge amount, on flexibility.[15] "If you ask people, do you prefer flexibility? Of course, everyone would say yes, they prefer flexibility," Mas told me in an interview. "But when you pose it as, 'You can choose a job where you get paid less, do you want to take that?' That's a different scenario. It's rubber meets the road at that point, and people, at least [according to] what we found, largely say no."[16]

CHAPTER 8

DON'T CALL US

THE ONLINE APPLICATION INVOLVED A QUIZ: "WHAT WOULD you do if you found $10 on a table and there was no note indicating what it is for?"

A. Take it, since it's meant to be a tip
B. Leave it where it is, since you don't know if it was meant for you
C. Ask the client if the money is a tip

The right answer was obvious to me: leave the money and do not ask questions.

"Say you wanted to work 8 hours on Monday. On Monday morning, you realize you only have 2 hours of work scheduled. What would you do?"

A. Cancel the job since it's not worth the commute
B. Complete the job since you committed to the job already
C. Call the support team and say you can only do it if you are given another job

"Complete the job" seemed to be the right answer, even if it meant traveling longer than you'd work.

"What is your opinion on taking personal calls when in a client's home?"

A. I always take personal calls
B. I take personal calls only if the client is in a different room
C. I never take personal calls

Not on company time!

The gig economy company that administered this quiz was hoping to sign up new cleaners in New York City in 2015. I had responded to its Craigslist ad, which read, "We're looking for high quality independent cleaning professionals" and "Income potential is up to $22/hr when working; set your own schedule and work as much as you'd like. Many of our top active cleaning professionals make $1,000+ per week!"

After entering my own name, address, and cleaning experience, I was referred to the quiz as part of my application.

Traditional freelancing relationships are fairly clear-cut. Independent workers take on projects that they can complete, well, independently. In the gig economy, companies like Upwork facilitate this type of work: Clients hand over assignments to workers, who complete them without any guidance from Upwork.

But with the arrival of Uber and "Uber for X" startups, an inherent conflict emerged. On one hand, these companies wanted to develop a reputation for providing great service, so that customers would begin to rely on them. On the other, their lawyers advised them that providing independent contractors with training, uniforms, benefits, or regular work shifts—that is, the things that produce happy, well-trained employees—could put the companies at risk of being sued for misclassifying employees as independent contractors.

Gig economy companies were in a pickle. They wanted to provide good service, but also to avoid accusations that they were treating their independent contractors like employees. Not training workers or setting expectations at all would lead to inconsistent service. And scheduling them to serve the same customers every week, motivating them with good benefits, and coaching them on how to improve put the companies at risk of lawsuits, which could force them to make an expensive shift to employees.

In the United States, there's no single test that determines whether workers are independent contractors or employees—it's different in different states and under different laws. And similarly in Europe, laws are often so complicated that there's no clear-cut way to define who is truly independent. Generally speaking, independent contractors should decide how to complete work, have potential for profit or loss, and, because they take on these responsibilities, have some bargaining power in contracts with other businesses. But are your particular workers being treated like employees? It will probably take a lawsuit to say for sure.

This gray area makes it difficult to understand how to classify employees and easy for companies to push the limits of the independent contractor classification. And it's tempting to push it to the point of what might reasonably be seen as cheating: to call workers "independent contractors" while still exercising employment-like control that doesn't give them the true autonomy to benefit from being their own bosses. The IRS estimates that companies misclassify millions of workers in this way.[1]

David Weil, who led the US Department of Labor's Wage and Hour Division during the Obama administration, recounts a typical scenario: "Week after week, it seemed, I was witness to an investigation from our district offices involving the incorrect classification of all types of workers: janitors, home health aides, drywall workers, cable installers, cooks, port truck drivers, and loading dock workers in distribution centers. In one telling case, construction workers went home at the end of the week as employees only to be informed on the following Monday that, perhaps by the magic of some unknown force, they had become 'member/owners' of hundreds of limited liability companies, effectively stripping them of federal and state job protections."[2]

Why didn't gig economy companies just reclassify everyone as an employee to avoid an accusation of misclassification?

There's no law preventing companies from offering employees the same type of flexibility that they offer their independent workforces. But a 2015 analysis by *Fortune* determined that if Uber were forced to do so, it would cost the company an additional *$4.1 billion* each year (a spokesperson told the magazine that the costs would be hard to calculate, as the business model would likely change). According to court documents from a 2016 lawsuit with the ride-hailing company Lyft, the company would have owed its drivers in California alone $126 million for the previous four years of work if it had hired them as drivers (Lyft disputes this number, saying that the amount assumes all of its drivers would be considered employees, even though many drove fewer than 60 hours over the four-year period).[3]

These were not the unit economics for which investors had signed up. Zirtual, a company that provided virtual assistants, said one reason it laid off hundreds of workers in 2015 was because it had switched from independent contractors to employees (the company was acquired soon after the switch). "All of these on-demand shared economy companies that have been built up all have independent contractors," its cofounder told *Bloomberg*. "Their model will be destroyed if they have to move contractors to employees."[4]

Gig economy companies were often left doing the equivalent of verbal and technical gymnastics—attempting to manage workers using strategies like creative quizzes without crossing over into treating them like employees. Pulling it off required a carefully orchestrated series of nods and winks. "We had to be very indirect about it," Katie Shea, the former New York City general manager of the now-defunct gig economy cleaning company Homejoy, explained to me. "We had to be like, we can't tell you what to do, but we can tell you that other cleaners who have done this have gotten five stars."[5] All of this seemed necessary to avoid what gig economy companies saw as archaic laws—which had been put into place long before anyone had imagined they'd find work with a smartphone.

After passing the cleaning company's quiz, I and other potential cleaners were invited to an orientation session on the sixth floor of a grubby building in Midtown Manhattan. About 20 people sat in a tiny room with cheap plastic school desks. They'd all been screened by phone. Most were African American, and many were dressed for an interview in blazers and black slacks.

A New York City manager whom I'll call Carol (not her real name) ran the orientation and adopted the tone of a grade-school teacher, frequently asking for class participation in order to keep attention. She played a video from an exemplary worker. "I like being a contractor with [the company] because it's being my own boss," she said. "Who doesn't want to spend time with their family?" The cleaner explained that she likes to leave behind white lilies, which she purchases herself, when she finishes every job.

"So what did we learn?" Carol asked the class.

As people responded, she rephrased and repeated their answers.

"You can work on your own, you're an independent contractor."

"She's passionate about her job."

Carol chirpily stated the obvious. "It's easy to find people to do physical labor, but what we want is people like [her]."

As Carol introduced the class to the app that would manage their schedules, "the lifeblood of your business," she continued to sell the job. One of the great things about it, she explained, was that we could work in any of the 37 cities in which the company operated: "If you want to get out of New York in the winter and go hang out in Miami, you can do that. If you want to take your kids on a Disney World vacation and pick up a few jobs along the way, you can do that." None of those vacation days would be paid, of course.

"What makes [this company] different?" Carol asked.

A man in a neat white shirt toward the back of the classroom raised his hand. "There's an open schedule, so you can work when you want."

Carol responded with a question. "Do you know Uber?" she asked. "We're like Uber for the home."

She started another video, this one in which the featured cleaner had a British accent. "Being an independent contractor, for me, it just means freedom and flexibility," a version of the previously featured woman explained.

Next Carol flipped to slides that explained how the cleaners would be paid. Clients would leave feedback, she told us, something we could "print out and hang on the fridge" if we wanted. But also, those ratings would impact our pay.

Workers started at $15 per hour, which is not a bad wage if you're not counting the time that it takes to travel between jobs or the cost of your cleaning supplies. With about a week's worth of good performance, that could jump to $17. The highest paid cleaners—those who worked the most hours and got the best reviews—made $22 per hour. Carol explained that because of this rating system, it was better to do a good job than to take as many jobs as possible.

She continued to explain the gig. Cleaners would get a $50 referral fee for signing up a friend and a $5 bonus for repeat business if a client requested them specifically. Though Carol didn't acknowledge it, this slide of her presentation came with the warning that "attempting to remove customers will result in immediate removal from the platform." You may be your own business, but these are not your own clients.

Slowly she started to roll out more of the bad news.

Those bright blue roller bags stacked at the back of the room? They had everything cleaners needed to get started, including a vacuum cleaner and a mop. But their cost—$150—would be deducted from checks, which meant working five jobs at the starting rate for free (a spokesperson for the company told me it has since stopped this practice). Carol did what she could to keep the conversation about supplies in "independent contractor" territory: "These are optional to take; this is your business, you are responsible for supplies."

Along with cleaning supplies, the bag held branded blue marketing materials, including cards cleaners could leave behind with their names on them, a checklist of tasks completed, and, Carol's favorite, branded stickers to put on the toilet paper after cleaners folded the ends into triangles.

Not only would the startup get its cleaners to distribute marketing materials throughout houses, it would also get them to purchase those marketing materials.

Later on in the orientation, a man in the front row raised his hand to clarify: "So if we run out of supplies, we have to buy them?"

Carol didn't elaborate or offer any sort of apology, but rather answered him without hesitation as though the answer should be obvious. "Of course."

More bad news: If a cleaner canceled a job between 2 and 36 hours in advance, his pay would be docked $15. If it was between 0 and 2 hours in advance, his pay would be docked for the cost of the job. It seemed harsh, but the company didn't really have another sound way of making sure cleaners showed up. It couldn't, and didn't, have supervisors to reprimand or coach its cleaners—to do so might suggest the kind of relationship that would make them employees. On the upside, customers were managed similarly: If they canceled within those same time windows, the cleaner got the extra amounts.

What about an emergency? asked another candidate. Carol's response: "You can dispute that through the help center." Something about the way she said it gave me the impression that the help center might not be so helpful.

It was time for another test, which members of the class took by navigating to a hyperlink on their mobile phones. As Carol left the room to grade the tests, she told the cleaners to pull their desks into small circles and "teach each other something." A mother who worked full-time at the parks department and wanted to pick up extra jobs on the side said she had worked as a housekeeper before, and her advice was to always ask the customer before doing anything, because people always have different ideas about what is right and wrong. A man who used to work at a gym had some tips about squeegeeing windows. A young girl who used to work at Old Navy taught her group about crocheting. The key was to "make a pretzel."

Did she have any cleaning experience? "Too much experience," she said. She also had a journalism degree and had completed half of a nursing program before running out of tuition money.

When Carol came back into the room, she dismissed two people who hadn't passed the test. Were there any questions? There were: What if we find an infestation of bed bugs? What if we're cleaning a home when someone is doing something behind their spouse's back that we feel uncomfortable with?

Carol responded that we were getting into a lot of "what if" territory, and, returning to her class participation schtick, asked what the cleaners thought they should do if they ran into a problem. The answer she was looking for was "navigate to the help section of the app." There, we would find answers to common complaints, such as "I feel uncomfortable or unsafe" (remove yourself from the situation and call the police) and instructions for what to do if a customer locked them out of the home by accident, or if they wanted to dispute a fee the company had taken from their pay for missing a scheduled cleaning or other violations to the terms of service.

"We'll call you!" shouted a woman wearing a skirt in the front row.

"Don't call us," Carol automatically corrected.

Uber was extremely shrewd at finding new ways to manage independent contractors through its app. "Employing hundreds of social scientists and data scientists," wrote the *New York Times* in 2017, "Uber has experimented with video game techniques, graphics and noncash rewards of little value that can prod drivers into working longer and harder—and sometimes at hours and locations that are less lucrative for them."[6]

One strategy was its surge pricing model, which made rates higher during busy times in order to encourage more drivers to work during those periods. According to a case study published in the *International Journal of Communication* in 2016, Uber used this model to request that drivers work during particular hours, sending them messages such as:

Are you sure you want to go offline? Demand is very high in your area. Make more money. Don't stop now!

UBER ALERT: Happy hour demand is extremely high right now! Log into your app and take advantage of the extra earnings. #UberOn.

We also want to remind you that we predict New Year's Eve will be the busiest night of the year. With such high demand, it will be a great night to go out and drive![7]

Surge pricing encouraged drivers to work at certain times. The way that Uber routed jobs to drivers encouraged them to take every request, regardless of how profitable the ride would be. Uber's minimum fare at the time of the study was around $5, which after Uber's commission meant that for short trips drivers would take home around $3, before accounting for expenses like gas and oil changes. Because drivers had few details when they decided to accept an Uber rider, they couldn't avoid these short trips.

They also had no way to know, before they accepted a job, whether it would lead them far away from a city without any hope of finding a fare for the way home. And once they accepted a job, Uber strongly discouraged them from canceling it. If they canceled too many trips, Uber would deactivate them.

Then there were "guaranteed fares," hourly wages that Uber offered to some drivers when it wanted them to work during rush hour or big events. At these times, Uber would pay a higher rate, similar to surge pricing, but drivers often had to commit to working in advance. "[The] language of opt-in or RSVP buffers the narrative of freedom and choice that Uber promotes to its drivers, while simultaneously masking a hierarchy in which select drivers are invited to earn more based on opaque criteria," the case study explained. "Drivers have the freedom to drive at 'flexible' hours at lower rates, but their flexibility is tailored to and dependent on demand as well as on the viability of base rates."

All of this made it difficult for a driver to understand how much he or she would make in a given week. Adding to this confusion, Uber changed fares frequently and without warning. For a long time drivers were paid based on a percentage of the total fare, so when fares dropped, they earned less per mile. In Kansas City, where Abe lived, one seasonal price cut, in January 2015, lowered the price of a 19-mile trip from the airport to downtown from about $38 to $22.[8] The company made similar price reductions in 47 other cities around the same time. It offered "guaranteed earnings" to counteract the rate cuts.[9] But to earn those guaranteed wages, drivers needed to accept 90% of ride requests and be online 50 out of every 60 minutes worked.[10] Essentially, they had to work for Uber exclusively—which hadn't been part of Uber's initial pitch of independence.

Also missing from Uber's pitch were the expenses. In May 2014, Uber advertised that its UberX drivers (those without a luxury sedan or SUV) made more than $90,000 in New York and more than $74,000 in San Francisco ("UberX driver partners are small business entrepreneurs demonstrating across the country that being a driver is sustainable and profit-able," the company wrote on its newsroom blog).[11] The adver-tised income led the perhaps overly credulous *Washington Post* to conclude, in a headline, "Uber's remarkable growth could end the era of poorly paid cab drivers."[12]

But Uber's estimation of its drivers' wages didn't include the significant cost of doing business, a cost that caught Abe, the Uber driver in Kansas City, and other Uber drivers by sur-prise. Uber drivers buy gas and spend money on insurance and car payments, and the company doesn't reimburse them. "I wasn't counting on expenses being all this much," Abe said. "An oil change at least once a month, car washes—you don't have to get a car wash, but if you're picking up someone in a dirty car, it's not professional—everything, the gas, air fresh-eners, they just add up really fast. I didn't realize at first, but it's literally less than minimum wage, after expenses." Abe calculated that driving cost him about 58 cents per mile (adopting the IRS's 2015 estimate for deductions related to business-related driving). In some cases, Uber charged customers 80 cents per mile. Then it took a commission that generally ranged between 20% and 30% and charged the pas-senger a booking fee that effectively made its commission higher. "It took me awhile to realize that the money I was making wasn't all mine," Abe said. "They trick you."

Internally, Uber *had* estimated what its drivers were actu-ally taking home after they'd paid for gas and other maintenance costs, and the result painted a much less sexy picture than the one it presented publicly. After its pricing model leaked to the press, Uber shared its internal calculations for drivers' wages minus expenses. On average, it estimated they were making $10.75 per hour in the Houston area, $8.77 per hour in Detroit, and $13.17 in Denver, which was slightly less than Walmart's average full-time hourly rate in 2016.[13] Based on the pricing model data, BuzzFeed determined that gas, insurance, and other costs of doing business amounted to about 22% of full-time drivers' gross pay in Denver, 24% in Houston, and 31% in Detroit.[14] Wages in all three markets cleared the minimum-wage, but not by much. And unlike a minimum-wage job, driving for Uber came without any paid breaks or benefits like health insurance. What it paid could change any time.

As Uber was pitching its company as a way to start a mini-business, internal presentations (which would eventually also leak to the press) showed that it considered the biggest competitor to its gig-based jobs to be McDonald's.[15] In January 2017, the company agreed to pay the Federal Trade Commission (FTC) $20 million to settle charges that it misled prospective drivers by exaggerating how much money they would make.[16]

Some drivers were still content with the service, despite the gap between its advertised opportunity and its actual pay. It was still work, and as Uber advertised, it could fit between other commitments like school or caring for children. Other drivers, who had signed up to finance their cars through Uber, felt that Uber had made it impossible to quit. As the company lowered rates, a bigger and bigger portion of their per-mile earnings was automatically deducted from their checks to pay for the car they'd acquired to do the job. "I just felt like I was trapped, like I was an Uber slave," one driver with such a set-up told *The Guardian*. She had ended up living out of her car. "It's just been a domino effect," she said. "It's really ruined my life."[17]

To someone like Abe, who had joined Uber believing it would make him independently wealthy, the reality of working for the company was especially disappointing. He wasn't trying to make a full-time living by driving for Uber (more than half of workers in the gig economy use it as a source of supplemental income[18]), but he still wanted to be treated fairly. As with GIN, the pyramid scheme that had cost him thousands of dollars, he felt as though an organization had misled him with a promise too good to be true. And as with GIN, he didn't plan to stay quiet about it.

When Abe figured out he'd been cheated by the GIN pyramid scheme, he emailed an investigative reporter at a local television station, who then obtained complaints similar to Abe's from the FTC and broke the story about the scam ("It was bizazro," the reporter, Ryan Kath, confirmed). It quickly became a national story. An ABC show called *The Lookout* flew Abe to Chicago, where GIN was located, and picked him up from the airport in a $230,000 Bentley that had previously been driven by GIN founder Kevin Trudeau himself.[19] Abe, dressed in a suit with a red checkered pocket handkerchief that matched his tie—and unbeknownst to his ABC hosts, slightly buzzed from a couple of drinks he'd downed to calm his nerves—helped them knock on the doors of the GIN office and one of Trudeau's alleged homes, a 14,000-square-foot mansion. Unsurprisingly, nobody answered either door. Then they let him drive. "It's got 600 horsepower, Abe," one of the show's anchors told him as he took the wheel, grinning.

"That was the best day of my life," Abe told me.

Now feeling duped by Uber, Abe would use a similar strategy. "KC [Kansas City] UBER DRIVERS: The time has come to unite as one voice!" he wrote on his Uber Freedom Facebook page in July 2015. "We need to make a stand and unite as one and tell Uber, enough is enough! Join the organization that will ensure KC drivers are treated fairly." Ten days earlier, he wrote, Uber had lowered rates in Atlanta by 22%, the first big cut in the short time Abe had been driving for Uber. "What is stopping them from lowering them [here]?" Abe asked.

Around the same time, Uber deactivated Abe. The company hadn't, according to Abe, provided an explanation, but he believed the decision was made in retaliation for his organizing activities (rather than, say, as a reaction to his habit of shotgunning rides). So he started collecting evidence for a lawsuit that would argue to the National Labor Relations Board that he and other drivers were being treated not as independent contractors, but as employees. It would be one of more than 15 such cases filed against Uber in 2015 and 2016.

When I met with Abe in July 2016, he was enthusiastic about his claim. At a Panera Bread restaurant in Kansas City, he pulled out a clear plastic folder holding Uber's code of conduct. "This is something you send to an employee, not an independent contractor," he said. Then he produced another stack of papers that contained the weekly summaries of his work with the company. On the bottom of the page, each summary showed a chart of "busy hours," with the outline of a black car placed as a marker in the grid to show the hours when he worked. "Last week you drove 6 of 16 busy hours," read one. "You could earn up to $260 more."

"They're not allowed to tell you to work, but these are insinuations that you should be working these hours," Abe said.

As the table between us filled with papers, Abe pointed to evidence that other drivers had sent him. Uber had told one driver to stop messaging passengers too much. Another it scolded for accepting cash payments instead of transacting through the app. A third it sent a "high cancellation warning," meaning the driver had canceled too many trips after accepting them and was at risk of being deactivated. Someone even got a warning because they'd been inactive on the platform. It said they would be deactivated if they didn't work again soon.

The various strategies companies used to direct gig economy workers may have felt to entrepreneurs like adapting a new innovation to a flawed system, but it struck many others as an old-fashioned way to avoid taxes and benefits.

Coordinating independent workers through an app, to many labor lawyers, looked a lot like the old process of cheating workers by misclassifying them. In January 2015, workers for Instacart, a gig economy company that sent independent contractors shopping on behalf of its customers, filed a lawsuit that alleged the company's employment practices were "unethical, oppressive and unscrupulous" (the case was subsequently settled). In March 2015, on the day after gig economy courier service Postmates announced its deal to deliver for Starbucks, its workers filed a similar class action lawsuit in California (which at the time of this writing was still ongoing). Workers for a food delivery service, Try Caviar, and the cleaning service Homejoy, did the same (Try Caviar's case was settled). By July 2016, Uber, the gig economy poster child, was fighting more than 70 lawsuits in federal courts—including many that alleged misclassification.[20]

Soon it was difficult to find any company that brokered independent workers and didn't have a lawsuit on its hands.

The gig economy had been born as a solution for the business problem of scaling a service business with venture capital. It had been promoted as a solution to economic woes. In 2014 and 2015, the gig economy started to look not like an innovation, but the continuation of a long change in how companies structured their workforces. Not a solution, but a problem in need of one.

Categories like temp worker and independent contractor put divisions between companies and workers who provide them with labor. Gig economy apps widened these divisions.

Without the need to manage people face-to-face, the relationship between a brand and its workers ceased to be a human relationship at all.

Mechanical Turk perhaps best exemplified this removal of the human interaction between employers and workers. The first "Mechanical Turk" was an eighteenth-century "automated" chess-playing contraption that, unbeknownst to its opponents, was actually manipulated by a fellow human chess player who directed each move. The modern Mechanical Turk didn't play chess, but it did allow for a similar exaggeration of technical abilities.

When companies could not yet accomplish some magic technology using code, they sometimes did so by automatically routing tasks to Mechanical Turk workers. Though Mechanical Turkers like Kristy had no way of knowing for sure for whom they were working, they were pretty sure that the account SergeySchmidt, a combination of the names of Google's founder and its former CEO, which only posted tasks involving videos from Google's video service YouTube, belonged to that company. And they were pretty sure that the JackStone account, which used a combination of the names of Twitter founders Jack Dorsey and Biz Stone, belonged to Twitter. Task by task, the workers helped technology companies like these "automatically" identify images, moderate comments, and accomplish other impressive feats that computers could not yet effectively handle on their own.

An entrepreneur once pitched me an app that provided nutritional information for any food based on a photo. He was very secretive about this technology that could identify the difference between an apple or a plum or a plate of spaghetti and look up the calorie content in a database. Sure enough, I found a task on Mechanical Turk that asked workers to identify the food in a photograph. That's how the app worked: humans. But it was supposed to look like magic. And Amazon's site so effectively created this impression that the people who hired Mechanical Turk workers sometimes forgot about their humanness altogether. As one group of researchers put it, the design of the site itself "allowed employers [to] see themselves as builders of innovative technologies, rather than employers unconcerned with working conditions."[21]

There were times when Kristy stumbled into emotionally taxing work that in a regular workplace would have come with preparation and consent. On one such occasion, she opened a task to find a slideshow of still shots taken from ISIS videos: people kneeling next to an explosive wire, preparing to die. A wicker basket full of human heads. It came with instructions similar to any other photo tagging job. Another slideshow contained photos of animal abuse so graphic that years later Kristy had trouble taking her dogs to the vet without crying.

The only indication that something exceptionally graphic could be found inside of a task was often an "adult only" qualification. Employers used this designation on any jobs that involved user-generated content that they couldn't control. Such jobs could pay well, and they most often didn't contain anything disturbing. Kristy considered them worth taking.

And so she accepted that psychological stress would be part of the job.

So, too, would physical stress. Kristy ignored a small, hard bump that developed on her wrist until it started to grow. It got a little bigger every day, until eventually it was the size of a marble and interfering with the way she held her mouse. When she finally went to the doctor, she learned that it was a ganglion cyst. He recommended surgery, but that would mean post-surgery prescriptions not covered by Canada's state health insurance. Another traditional treatment for "Bible bumps," as they are sometimes called, is to hit them with a heavy book. And so one day, when she couldn't stand it anymore, Kristy gave the bump a good bashing.

Eventually the pain went away. Then a new pain appeared, up her wrist, toward her elbow. A neurologist told her that it was carpal tunnel and a repetitive strain injury. The ideal response would have been rest. But there is no workers' compensation in the gig economy. There is no paid sick leave in the gig economy. And among US workers who rely on sites like Mechanical Turk for their entire income, almost 40% don't have health insurance.[22] Kristy wore a wrist brace and an elbow brace and kept on clicking.

Mechanical Turk was the only option when Kristy's family needed money quickly. It allowed her husband to go back to high school to get his diploma. And it allowed her to earn an income from home without a college degree or a thick resume. She made it work.

But when her husband finally landed a job, as a forklift

driver at a printer company, she told him she never wanted to depend on Mechanical Turk again.

Shortly later, she applied for university.

Every night after he taught his gig economy classes in Dumas, Arkansas, Terrence went home and cooked dinner for his grandmother. Then he went on a long walk and contemplated what might end the cycle of poverty in Dumas.

From the first class he'd taught for Samasource, it had been clear to him that the gig economy alone was not the answer.

The curriculum called for instruction on how to build an online portfolio, how to tell which Upwork jobs were scams and which were real, and how to use the platform itself. He could see how someone might reasonably believe that leveling the employment playing field meant teaching Dumas residents the ins and outs of an online job platform—Terrence even believed it at first. But he had come to more fully appreciate how drastically uneven Dumas's patch of the playing field really was.

Fifteen percent of adults in Dumas had never graduated high school. Terrence was trying to teach some of his students how to write an online resume profile when they hadn't been taught to write persuasively at all. He was trying to teach them to decipher online job postings when they struggled with reading comprehension. Some Dumas residents were so unfamiliar with computers in general that they didn't know where to type in the URL on a search browser, or how to send an email.

According to a final report Samasource submitted to the Dumas program's main backer, 60% of the students who took Terrence's class did not own a computer, and 44% of them did not have access to the internet, even on their phones.[23]

Then there were the skills that came so standard in affluent areas that people forgot they were indeed skills that needed to be taught and learned, just like any others. Most of Terrence's students hadn't been taught how to learn, and they hadn't done anything academic since leaving high school. Terrence knew that applying for jobs was intimidating for anyone, but much more intimidating for people who had experienced the consistent setbacks of poverty. And it was harder still to keep applying after hearing "no" over and over and over again, which they inevitably did when they started to submit resumes on Upwork.

Jobs on Upwork, Terrence quickly learned, tended to be either those that didn't require any qualifications—which were won by workers in other countries willing to work for $3 or $5 per hour—or those that were extremely specialized and well remunerated, but went to workers with college and even master's degrees. This contrast of very-low-paying work and very-high-paying work could be observed in Upwork's decision to set a minimum wage (it decided on $3 per hour) while some of its workers wrote blog posts about making $1,000 per week using the platform.[24]

Terrence knew it was true that more jobs were shifting to the gig economy. He knew that the gig economy enabled flexible jobs and could be a provider of supplemental income for people who otherwise wouldn't have been able to make ends meet. But the Silicon Valley idea that the internet would be an equal opportunity employer, that anyone could turn on employment as though it were a water faucet, didn't really work out for people living in Dumas. Rather, it had the opposite effect: It created international competition for jobs, even some local ones that the people of Dumas would have had to themselves without the internet.

Dumas wasn't unique in this regard. In a preliminary study, NYU Stern School of Business professor Arun Sundararajan plotted the hourly wages of workers in the San Francisco Bay Area who found jobs through the odd jobs website Task-Rabbit against the Bureau of Labor Statistics's average wage rates for the same area. He found that workers who won gigs online actually earned more than their offline peers when the job required a physical presence, such as electrical work or carpentry. His hypothesis was that because the gig economy website made it less of a hassle to find workers to complete these jobs, more people sought services, which pushed wages up. For digital-only tasks like graphic design or writing, however, wages of Bay Area gig workers were lower than those of their peers who found gigs offline. Though they lived in one of the most expensive areas in the United States, online, they were competing with workers everywhere.[25]

Kristy found the same problem when she experimented with Upwork. "I found a race to the bottom," she said. "I couldn't compete with people living in countries where the income was lower, but the education was the same and their experience was the same."

I found the same problem when I tried to make it in the gig economy while reporting for a magazine story.

"Furloughed? Try Freelancing on Fiverr," advised a Yahoo news headline during the government shutdown of 2013.[26] Fiverr was so named because, at launch, it asked workers to offer their services for a flat rate of $5 (workers now can set different rates). You could use Fiverr, the startup's founder explained, to make money doing what you love in your spare time. Like 75% of people surveyed in a Fiverr-sponsored poll, the deal sounded pretty good to me.[27] But that was before I realized that 4,786 other workers on Fiverr had, like me, offered to proofread papers for $5. My profile was nowhere to be found among the first several pages of the site's search results for the service. To all but the most persistent of potential employers, I was invisible.

I finally found work on TaskRabbit, where, at the time, workers could bid on odd job requests posted by their neighbors. But to get those gigs, I used advantages that Terrence's students didn't have. In frantic messages to prospective employers, I name-dropped my university, explained that I used to have a job helping high school kids edit their college admissions essays, and joked about how six years of experience as a swimming instructor had given me exceptional patience. As with most things, having led a privileged life was very helpful. As was being white. Researchers at Stanford University found in a study that an online posting for a physical item received 13% fewer responses and 17% fewer offers when the item was held by a black hand than when it was held by a white hand—and that was when selling something as simple as an iPod.[28] Most of Terrence's students were African American. Most online work platforms show employers profile photos of applicants.

Applying for gigs on platforms like Upwork was just like applying for any job. It took a lot of effort, and it was rife with similar discrimination and sources of inequality.

To Terrence's students, the constant failure to get gigs was paralyzing. Spending hours applying for gigs to no avail is one thing when you're not desperate for money and pretty sure that you have other options. All work and no pay is an entirely different experience when you can't afford to work for free.

Shakira Green, a 28-year-old certified nursing assistant, took the Samaschool class in the hope of finding a job that would allow her to work during the day, when her daughter was in school, rather than on her overnight shift. "When the class finished, I did, every day, apply for jobs and apply for jobs, but after a while of applying and not really landing any jobs, I kind of just gave up on it, to be honest," she told me. "I think I just got frustrated, and I got tired of always writing publications, submitting proposals, and just not getting any feedback."

Even when Terrence helped students with their portfolios, they almost never got an interview.

One student landed a customer service job at $7 per hour.

A few tried working for $3 or $5 per hour. Someone found a $50 project, but it took so many hours to actually accomplish that the hourly pay became meaningless.

At the end of Terrence's first course, the feedback was consistent: This is a nice platform and all, but we're spending a lot of time working on it without getting paid. Where are the jobs?

Even his students who succeeded in the gig economy, like Gary, who had gotten a job taking customer service calls, still felt as though their income was precarious and their lives were insecure. Part of the problem was that the gig economy's much-ballyhooed flexibility often seemed to apply more to the company than to the employee. Gary's job offer letter had mandated that he work a "minimum of 30 hours per week." But it turned out this had been a one-sided commitment. When there was enough work to do, Gary was obligated to work at least 30 hours per week. When there was not enough work to do, he might only be able to get 10 or 20 hours worth of work. He never knew when hours would be available, which meant that he couldn't commit to another job outside of the call center.

In July, when he'd first started the remote call center job, this hadn't seemed like a problem. Because he took calls about broken air conditioners, there was more than enough work to do during the summer heat. When he couldn't work 30 hours or didn't want to, he had to let his boss know in advance so that his absence wouldn't impact his rating as a contractor.

When summer turned to fall, though, Gary started to realize he was in trouble. Still a couple of months away from broken heater season, he fretted about how many hours he would work the next week as the majority of the country enjoyed a temperate climate.

Gary and other virtual call center contractors picked their hours on a rolling basis, with the highest rated among them choosing first. Hours were usually released every two weeks, but as time went on, fewer and fewer were available. Gary was lucky to get 15 hours each week. If someone else forfeited their hours in order to attend a doctor appointment or something unexpected, he could sometimes pick up a few more. "You scramble," he said. "You check the board constantly, like every hour [you're looking]. For a half hour here, a half hour there, to try to collect extra hours."

During the month he spent training without pay, Gary hadn't been able to pay his bills. Now he didn't have any savings to fill in the gaps between periods when he could get work with the call center.

Whatever happened, Gary knew that some had it worse. He'd kept in touch with a few of the other call center workers who had been in his virtual training course. Some told him they were being paid $3 or $4 per hour, which meant their managers—most likely also contractors—were keeping a large percentage of their wages for themselves. It wasn't as though an employment relationship would necessarily have prevented wage theft. But in the gig economy, paying $3 or $4 per hour to independent contractors was legal (as long as you were truly treating them as independent workers). They were not protected by minimum wage laws, which in 2016 mandated $8.00 per hour in Arkansas. "I don't care how many hours you're getting," Gary said. "$3 per hour does not pay bills."

Terrence agreed. Samaschool was teaching people to apply for jobs, but it was difficult to actually get the job without the requisite skills. So Terrence made a suggestion for the next class cohort: Teach students not only how to use Upwork, the gig economy platform, and how to promote themselves, but also some skills that could help land a job. Samasource agreed on the strategy, and Terrence taught classes on virtual assistance, customer service, and social media marketing to the students who signed up for his next ten-week course. Still, only 2 of 21 people who enrolled found virtual work.

For the next cohort of students, Samaschool decided that Terrence's class would focus on learning one particularly valuable skill. The organization had done an internal analysis to decide which skill it would be. Social media seemed like a sweet spot: Many small businesses recognized they didn't know how to use social media and didn't have a strategy around it. They were looking for part-time workers who spoke English as a first language, the work could be done remotely, and it paid relatively well.

The problem was that the job required constant creative thinking and meticulous writing skills, and these requirements did not match well with his students' experiences. "We've been doing physical labor," Terrence said, "where you get a job and obey what your boss tells you." This experience was, once again, a lot to overcome in a ten-week course. But the factory and retail work that many of his students were more accustomed to, Terrence knew, was in the process of disappearing. Sometimes when he went on his six-mile walks, he thought about this—about what might happen as machines continued to take over those jobs. What the hell was Dumas going to do? He wasn't ready to give up on the gig economy.

Samaschool adjusted its curriculum yet again. Rather than having students look for work on Upwork, Samaschool recruited small businesses to hire students as interns at the end of the program.

The arrangement was more motivating: Students got paid for their work ($300, most of which was paid by Samaschool), and they felt as though they were interviewing for a job. They developed social media strategies that Samaschool hoped the businesses would eventually hire them to execute. But after two rounds of classes and 13 graduates, just one student went on to complete additional work for the business at which she'd interned. Attendance and enrollment started to dwindle.

When I visited in late 2015, I arrived at one of Terrence's classes at 6:10 p.m. It was supposed to start at 6:00, but the big, interactive classroom was empty, and I found Terrence leaning on a railing outside.

"I don't understand what is happening," he told me. He had just hung up his cell phone after speaking with one of his students, who had a headache and wouldn't be coming to class. Another student was watching her son's football game. "This has never happened before," he continued, tears of frustration welling up in his eyes.

Terrence was the kind of teacher who counted the extra work he did in days rather than hours. Of course he had all of his students' cell phone numbers. And he started to vigorously put those numbers to work, dialing or texting as was age appropriate. He called a community college student first. Did she think that the curriculum was too hard? Were they cramming too much into one day? She thought so. He recorded the call to replay at a meeting with Samasource. A woman who worked at a tobacco superstore finally showed up to class—she was resting when Terrence telephoned and woke her up—and he asked her the same questions. She was a mother of five, she replied. Of course she could handle the curriculum.

Before I left Dumas, I went to the downtown pharmacy to buy a snack. I sat in a booth with a pickle and some potato chips and watched as white people came and left through the front door while black people used the back door. Every once in a while, someone interrupted the pattern. But though it was no longer mandated, it was still there.

An older black man wearing a purple plaid shirt shuffled in through the back door and picked up his prescription at the counter. "Is this seat taken?" he asked me. It was not, and he sat down.

He asked me if I was from "the North," and I said that I was. I asked him if he lived in Dumas, and he said he used to, until his landlord raised his rent and piled all of his belongings in his front room.

It is supposed to rain tonight, he said, and I asked him if that were a good thing—if the fields needed it. He responded by summing up the basic problem in the gig economy and the economy in general. "Some people got enough," he said of the rain. "Some people have too much. Some people don't have anything. That's just how it goes."

CHAPTER 9

THE GOOD JOBS STRATEGY

HAVING PIVOTED AWAY FROM CONDO MAINTENANCE JUST six weeks earlier, Managed by Q launched its office cleaning and handyman service in April 2014. Shortly later, Saman, Emma, and Dan began doubting whether the model they'd chosen—hiring subcontractors to do the cleaning—would work as well as they'd hoped.

Hiring independent contractors had proven to be a great strategy when it came to building the software part of Managed by Q. Saman had worked with a team of freelancers who lived in Argentina to create the first Managed by Q iPad app. They were easy to work with, and the app worked well. Ensuring the cleaning part was done well every day, though, had turned out to be more unpredictable.

Managed by Q had promised its clients detailed, personalized service. One of its "positive touchpoints," called "knolling," involved arranging every item on a desk in 90-degree angles, making it look like a well-organized tool bench. Office managers would, according to the pitch, see the same cleaners every day, and they'd be able to customize their service—for example, by indicating the way that their chairs should be arranged—through the iPads Managed by Q installed on their office walls.

As Managed by Q started cleaning its first offices, it learned that customers indeed wanted their chairs arranged in a particular way. They also wanted their pillows arranged a particular way on their lobby couches, and their coffee machine cleaned with a particular soap. Managed by Q communicated this feedback to its cleaning company's supervisors, but the messages didn't always translate into meticulous service.

Managed by Q had partnered with janitorial companies to provide office cleaning staff rather than hire workers directly. And to cleaning industry veterans, some of the requests its clients submitted looked nitpicky: In a 10,000-square-foot office, was Managed by Q really going to worry about the pillows?

After working all day at the Managed by Q office, Emma spent most of her evenings at clients' offices, checking to make sure that the cleaners had incorporated all of the feedback that companies submitted through their iPads (which had to be relayed to the cleaning companies' supervisors in emails). It wasn't just a matter of checking details that kept her busy. Sometimes cleaners didn't show up, and she'd have to call reliable cleaners to fill in for them. Sometimes nobody brought a mop, which meant a late-night trip to Home Depot.

All of this was a problem, because to make its business work, Managed by Q's service truly needed to be perfect. Saman, Dan, and Emma knew that most cleaning businesses had a lot of what the business world calls "churn." Customers quit frequently, and companies spent too much money trying to recruit new ones. This included gig economy cleaning businesses. Homejoy, for instance, reportedly spent a fortune on customer acquisition and struggled with customer retention. To attract customers, it advertised deals that sold its services at an extremely reduced rate, in some cases offering first-time home cleanings for the dirt-cheap rate of $19.99. That expensive investment in new customers didn't pay off. Journalist Christina Farr, at the time reporting for the website Backchannel, reviewed a third-party analysis of the company's financials that showed only about a quarter of Homejoy's customers continued to use the service after the first month, and fewer than 10% had stuck around for six months after they'd signed up.[1]

Part of the pitch Managed by Q had made to investors was that Managed by Q would do better. "No churn! No way!" became an unofficial company slogan. But the only way to combat churn was to keep customers happy. That proved more difficult than the entrepreneurs had anticipated: Managed by Q lost its biggest client after about a month. Around the same time, Emma and Managed by Q cut ties, and Dan took over cleaning operations.

Motivating "operators," what Managed by Q called its frontline workers, to do a better job became a priority. The first step was getting to know them. On a Saturday, the entrepreneurs invited everyone to the office for pizza. Saman and Dan gave updates on new iPad features (like one that provided photos of exactly how the pillows on the couch were to be arranged) and recognized operators who had performed well. By the second or third "assembly," instead of 10 to 20 cleaners, there were 60 to 70 of them. Dan and Saman raffled off prizes, including an iPad.

Getting to know the cleaners felt right to the founders, but it didn't automatically solve their problems. For one thing, the closer Managed by Q got with its cleaners, the more awkward it became with the cleaning companies, which felt the startup was overstepping its bounds. The operators weren't Managed by Q's employees, after all. And the assemblies weren't exactly making the service suddenly easy to run. Potential disasters still emerged with exhausting regularity.

In Emma's absence, Dan found himself spending a lot of time putting out fires. When a client suspected that a Managed by Q operator had drunk the company's liquor, he jumped on a motorcycle with a bottle of whisky. When another startup complained about how Managed by Q stored cleaning supplies at its office, Dan showed up on a weekend and built storage shelves. When cleaners didn't show up for work, he and Managed by Q's other first employees finished the day working at their own office and then went to clean for their clients at night.

Elsewhere, Uber-like companies were having similar trouble delivering a perfect experience. By the end of 2016, the Better Business Bureau in New York had received more than 350 complaints about Handy, a gig economy cleaning company, and 186 of them were related to problems with service. It wasn't that all of Handy's cleaners did a terrible job, but rather that customers didn't know what to expect. The startup's Yelp reviews swung back and forth from one extreme to the other. It had more than 2,000 five-out-of-five-star reviews and almost 1,000 one-star reviews, with some Yelpers raving about "Tito C." or "Ranu T." and others telling horror stories about theft, sporadic quality, and annoyance at different cleaners showing up every time.

Many "Uber for X" companies had, like Handy and Managed by Q, taken on services that were more complex than Uber's job of getting customers from point A to point B. Their workers stepped into people's homes to clean, picked up deliveries from restaurants that may or may not have been running on time, and completed a myriad of errands. It was more difficult for them to provide perfect service.

Assemblies had helped give Managed by Q a better idea of the challenges its operators faced and a way to provide some coaching, but they didn't meaningfully change their operators' jobs, which Managed by Q's founders were starting to suspect weren't great. Managed by Q finally asked the subcontractors what they paid their cleaners, and it turned out in some cases to be barely minimum wage. This was consistent with what Emma had learned when she'd cold-called dozens of subcontractors to recruit them as partners. Most were cagey about how much they paid their cleaners. They'd stumble over the amount, refuse to provide it, or say something like "Well, on the books or off the books?" It was clear that office cleaning work in New York, outside of the unionized jobs in skyscrapers, was not a great gig.

This was troubling to Dan and Saman for business

reasons—without controlling compensation, there were few good ways to motivate and train workers—but also for personal reasons. Neither Saman nor Dan was interested in starting a company that offered crappy, low-paying jobs.

Starting a tech company is very likely to involve stress, insane hours, and shattered dreams, and not very likely to succeed. A sense of bigger purpose is one of the more logical reasons for launching a startup, and it had been a factor for both Saman and Dan.

The advertising campaigns Saman had worked on before becoming an entrepreneur sometimes attracted attention. His most famous was the "Whopper Sacrifice," a Facebook app that rewarded people with a free Burger King sandwich if they "de-friended" ten people. But in 2009, as the United States slipped into a recession, Saman didn't feel he was doing anything meaningful by trying to get people to buy cars and hamburgers, and nothing drove this home like trying to describe these efforts to his grandmother. In order to translate a description of his projects into Farsi, he had to simplify them to their most basic components and language. Hearing them that way made them sound stupid.

It wasn't all altruistic, this desire to make an impact. It was more of a desire to make something permanent, as opposed to the ethereal ads he had been working on. It was at least partly driven by ego.

When Saman's wife got a work assignment in Japan, he had quit his advertising job and gone with her, and from their apartment in Tokyo, he had started a labor marketplace that launched in 2010. It was designed to "rid the world of unemployment" by connecting "Lawyers, Painters, Babysitters, Bakers, Photographers, Tutors, Typists, Copywriters, Plumbers, Party Planners, Programmers, Artists and Actors" with people who wanted to hire them. "While it's true that employment opportunities in the traditional sense are not what they used to be—and may never be again—there is still plenty of opportunity for motivated individuals with exceptional skills to build a sustainable and thriving freelance career," Saman told a tech blog.[2] It was the gig economy before anyone called it the gig economy. And like many pieces of the gig economy, it grew out of good intentions, and perhaps some naiveté. He named it Tischen, a take on a German word for "table" (and a name, he realized in retrospect, most of his target customers couldn't pronounce). Although Tischen never took off, the project had brought him into the world of entrepreneurship, where he'd felt at home ever since.

Dan, Saman's cofounder, had similarly been driven to startups by a mix of ego and a desire for meaningful impact.

This had started as a kid, when he told people that he wanted to be president. It had continued through high school, as he largely ignored his schoolwork and directed attention instead toward pursuits like protesting the class trip to Disney World (he'd read that Disney used sweatshop labor, so he planned a Habitat for Humanity trip instead).

The summer before he left for college in 2007, Dan drove with his girlfriend (a senior at Princeton) and his brother to hear then-senator Barack Obama speak at a concert venue in

Philadelphia. As Obama led the crowd in a chorus of "Happy Birthday" for the local celebrity who sang the national anthem, Dan was struck by the sense he was seeing a different kind of politician. Obama described a US population with families that "can't figure out if they should fill up the gas tank, or whether they can save for their retirement or for sending their children to college" and where 45 million people went without health insurance. He spoke of "a very simple idea that we all have simple obligations to each other." Dan found himself nodding along. "Instead of people taking responsibility," Obama said, "what we end up with is folks trying to blame somebody. Blaming the other party. Blaming immigrants. Blaming gay people. Always finding a reason for why we can't do something. And that is why I think so many people are turning out all across the country."[3]

Dan felt inspired. He wasn't the type to preach hope and change, but he wanted to make a difference, if for no other reason than he didn't really believe anyone else could do a better job. Hope and change were in the air. You could feel it. You could touch it. It confirmed his desire to become a politician who worked on social issues.

His first plan for after college was to join the military—become a naval officer before running for public office. He already had a start date for basic training when he fell for an opponent's fake during a rugby game, tore his ACL, MCL, and meniscus in a single fall, and ended up a paralegal in New York City instead. He didn't like working in law—making an impact was too slow of a process that involved much too much paperwork—and, by extension, he'd put his goal of entering politics on the sideline. But he still was interested in social issues.

Both Dan and Saman saw themselves as people who would make a positive social impact, and Managed by Q's current business strategy didn't necessarily fulfill that vision.

The answer to both the company's business problems and to its founders' cognitive dissonance was clearly to hire front-line workers. Not just hire them (there are plenty of terrible employers, too), but train them well, and pay them better.

The potential problem with this approach was funding. In August 2014, four months after launch, Managed by Q announced a $775,000 round of funding, which was enough to get by for some months before it would need to raise another round. At least one of its early investors had found the potential similarities between Managed by Q and Uber to be appealing. Scott Belsky had been an early investor in Uber, and he liked the idea that Managed by Q (by now just "Q" for short) would be a technology platform that brokered other people's labor and goods: a startup that could scale infinitely without much upfront investment. "I love businesses that replace the pipes and upgrade the user experience for some aspect of everyday living—I call these 'interface layer' businesses," Belsky told *Business Insider* at the time. "Uber did this for transportation. Shyp [another investment] is doing it for shipping. And Q is doing it for office/space management." He suggested that "the interface of Q" had the potential to "revolutionize many industries that operate underneath."[4]

Many investors were, like Belsky at the time, still enamored with the "Uber for X" strategy, and to keep them interested, Managed by Q would need to justify its decision to invest in jobs instead. It planned to compare this strategy to a company that was arguably just as successful as Uber. Starbucks had transformed the job of being a barista from a specialized version of the cashier into a hipster profession that involved benefits and a career path. Managed by Q's idea was to do the same for its "operators."

Dan knew somebody who knew an executive at Starbucks. Her name was Dervala Hanley, VP of global strategy at the time, and she was in the process of starting Starbucks's partnership with Arizona State University, which today covers tuition for all employees who want to pursue a bachelor's degree. The campaign, she would later write on her LinkedIn profile, earned two billion media impressions at launch and was mentioned by President Obama. Seeing the opportunity to meet someone who had done pathbreaking work in creating good jobs in the service sector, Dan asked for an introduction.

Dervala told Dan about a book called *The Good Jobs Strategy* by Zeynep Ton, a professor at MIT's business school. The book argues that offering good jobs can benefit a company's bottom line. Profiling companies like QuickTrip, UPS, Costco, and Trader Joe's, which profit by offering their employees good jobs, Ton wrote with power and passion about a different approach to business that matched what Managed by Q hoped to do.

You can certainly succeed at the expense of your employees by offering bad jobs—jobs that pay low wages, provide scant benefits and erratic work schedules, and are designed in a way that makes it hard for employees to perform well or find meaning and dignity in their work . . . Many people in the business world assume that bad jobs are necessary to keep costs down and prices low.

But there is another, and still profitable, choice, the book argues, one that involves providing decent pay, benefits, and stable work schedules.

These companies—despite spending much more on labor than their competitors do in order to have a well-paid, well-trained, well-motivated workforce—enjoy great success. Some are even spending all that extra money on labor while competing to offer the lowest prices—and they pull it off with excellent profits and growth.[5]

The key to making investment in labor work, Ton concluded, was operational efficiency. It wasn't enough to treat workers better. Companies also needed to empower those workers to deliver great customer service and help avoid expensive chaos. They needed to allow employees to break from standardized policies in order to adapt to customers' needs, expect employees to do different types of work during slow times instead of scheduling them sporadically, and staff their stores with more, not fewer, employees than they predicted they would need to do the job. Do these things, she argued, and the strategy could work even for stores with low prices, like the convenience store QuikTrip.

With Ton's model, because employees are trained well and stick around, they have enough knowledge to help customers. Because stores are not understaffed, they also have the time to do so. "They work harder and they work better," Ton wrote. "You get lower employee turnover, so you have people with more experience making fewer mistakes."[6] This was research-backed logic, not a hypothetical labor revolution like the gig economy. Dan would eventually meet Ton about a year into Managed by Q. "She is not a bleeding heart," he would determine, approvingly. He used her theory to build his case for employing workers.

Though Dan and Saman started with cleaning services, their plan was to build a dashboard that would allow an office manager to request anything from a light bulb change to a caterer by pushing a button. If a client was impressed with Managed by Q's cleaners and handymen, that relationship could become a gateway to sales for anything an office needed. But if Managed by Q sent out office operators who hated their jobs and did them halfheartedly, the company would be less likely to make those extra sales from its dashboard. Acquiring new customers could be expensive, and sending an employee who hadn't been vetted, trained, and incentivized by Managed by Q would be a good way to lose business.

Beyond that, providing good jobs could save Managed by
Q money recruiting cleaners. Gig economy companies often
struggled to retain their workers. According to one report by
Alison Griswold, a journalist at *Slate* at the time, former employees at Handy estimated that the company brought on 400
to 500 new cleaners every week, at a cost of hundreds of dollars each (Handy told the reporter its onboarding costs were
less than $100). The same report estimated that after 60
to 90 days, between 20% and 40% of those new cleaners
stopped taking jobs from Handy.[7] Which meant the hundreds
of dollars spent to onboard them had been wasted.

By contrast, very few people ever quit at companies that
used Ton's "Good Jobs Strategy." QuikTrip, one of her model
companies, had 13% of its staff leave each year, which was
wildly lower than the industry's 59% rate. Trader Joe's turnover rate among full-time employees was less than 10%, and
Costco employees who had worked at the company for more
than a year turned over at a 5.5% rate.[8]

Outside of Silicon Valley, the Good Jobs Strategy was a
less-than-shocking revelation. "This is M.B.A. 101 stuff," said
Diane Burton, a professor of human resource studies at
Cornell University, when the *New York Times* explained Managed by Q's strategy. "When people are your source of competitive advantage, it's clear that a long-term employment
relationship and what we would call a 'good job' is good for
the workers and good for the companies."[9] This is why some
US employers offer paid maternity leave, vacation leave, and

sick days despite having no legal obligation to do so—because they're competing to attract and retain employees.

But in the startup world, few companies had attempted this approach outside of their professional offices (where they took it to the extreme with free meals and on-site dry cleaning). As Dan explained this strategy to potential investors, some of them pushed back, pressuring him to switch to an Uber model. But others saw it as a wise decision.

The startup announced its seed round of funding, $1.65 million, in November 2014. It raised another $15 million in June 2015. "Our employees are our greatest strength, not a cost to be minimized," read an early tweet from the Managed by Q account, which linked to its new job application. "Come clean."

Managed by Q operators started at $12.50 per hour, compared to New York State's $9.00 minimum wage.[10] This wasn't as much as the estimate for Uber's average hourly wage, but according to New York State, it was much more than the pay for a typical janitor. Entry-level janitors in the state earned on average $21,000 per year or about $10 per hour, if they worked for 40 hours per week.[11] Nationwide, the average was $15,000 or around $7.00 per hour.[12]

Managed by Q's operators received a $0.25 per hour raise every six months. If they worked more than 30 hours per week, they received free health insurance, 40 hours of vacation, and a retirement savings plan.[13] Managed by Q also prioritized creating jobs that provided reliable work. The startup, which made most of its revenue from weekly office cleanings, didn't have unpredictable busy hours, like a store or Uber or Handy did, so workers could count on coming into work at the same times every week.

In addition to paying a higher wage than its competitors, Managed by Q also constructed a career path for operators. Some workers, like Anthony Knox, a 39-year-old father of three who was born in Harlem, took advantage of this opportunity to steadily rise through the company ranks.

Anthony had heard about Managed by Q while he was working at the Human Resources Administration, where he advised about 30 people every week about where they could get shelter, clothing, and a haircut before a job interview. A growing company, he hoped, would mean more opportunity. "It's how hard you work in life," he said. "That's part of who I am."

He submitted his resume, which detailed his experience working 11 years as a medical assistant and his nursing degree, and was immediately called in to attend an info session. There, he took a verbal quiz, answering questions such as "To clean this surface, would you spray it directly with product or use a rag?" (the right answer is to spray the rag first—you don't want to risk stray spray getting on someone's clothes or in their eyes), and then did two (paid) deep cleans as a test. Having performed well on both, he was given an office to clean. He still remembers the exact date he started, November 21, 2014. He earned $12.50 an hour and kept his job at the HRA, which meant that in a typical day he might travel from his home in the Bronx to his day job in Queens to a cleaning site in Brooklyn or Manhattan.

Back then, there were only a couple dozen field operators, and about ten office operators, so "everybody kind of knew everybody."

The office he cleaned first, which belonged to a professional services firm, was 17,000 square feet, and he cleaned it Monday through Thursday, and then again on Saturday. The first thing he did every day when he arrived was collect all of the dishes from the desks and put them in the dishwasher. While it ran for 45 minutes, he cleaned the kitchen. Then he put the dishes away and moved on to 103 desks, which each required dusting and a wet cloth. The men's bathroom had two stalls and three sinks. The women's bathroom had four stalls and three sinks, plus tiny wastebaskets for "women's stuff." He cleaned the walls, the toilets, the trash cans, and the Dyson air blowers. He did it all in 4.5 hours, after the offices had closed for the day, and his clients rated every cleaning with five stars.

After a few months, Managed by Q promoted Anthony to "mentor," which meant that while he cleaned, he showed new employees how to do the job. He taught them, for instance, to use pink rags in the bathroom, blue on glass and mirrors, and yellow in the kitchen; that you have to wet a Magic Eraser before it will work; and how to line a trash can properly. He got a raise to $14.00 an hour.

A couple of months after that, he was promoted to supervisor and made responsible for quality control on between 40 and 65 accounts. He started at $15.50 per hour. Every day, he went to Q to pick up keys and a schedule for checking the sites. He got them from the company supply closet, which was stacked from floor to ceiling with clear plastic tubs full of swag that the company handed out to its workers: Q-branded hats, T-shirts, jackets, sunglasses, lens cases. Anthony opened the key safe—mounted on a wall across from the swag—using his thumbprint. Inside were a colorful array of keychains, and red lights would blink next to the ones that he was scheduled to collect.

When I met him in August 2015, Anthony was one of about eight supervisors in New York whose fingers opened this safe. Later he delivered the keys to cleaners whom he "spot checked" for quality. If he found an error, he taught him or her what had gone wrong. If the client had feedback or there had been a change in service, he communicated it to the cleaners. Next, he wanted to run trainings. "You get to choose your own path," he said. "I like training people because when you show people the right way to do something, they usually do it right."

Or, he said, he would go the IT route. He would observe the company's engineers during his free time until he learned the job. "You don't need the degree," he told me. "As long as you have the skills, they will promote you. You don't really get a lot of employers where you can start as a cleaning operator and end up at the top of the company. You could go to McDonald's and start as a cashier, but it would take you a lot longer to work your way up to franchise owner."

By July 2015, Managed by Q had 228 accounts in New

York, 25 in Chicago, and 28 in San Francisco, and a customer retention rate over 90%. Customers spent almost 30% of their total monthly bill with Managed by Q on services other than their routine office cleaning, by adding on items like maintenance and cleaning supplies.[14] And the company had begun to get attention for its Good Jobs Strategy, which CNN called "the anti-Uber model."[15]

At the same time, the difficulties of applying the Uber model to businesses beyond transportation grew increasingly clear.

Homejoy, another gig economy cleaning company, announced it was going out of business in July 2015. Others followed: The companies that had pitched using the gig economy as a way to park cars in San Francisco either abruptly shifted their business or closed. On-demand laundry startup Washio, which had charged just $2.19 a pound for washing and folding clothing, plus delivery, announced it was calling it quits.[16] The number of venture capital investments in the gig economy fell from its peak of 179 deals in 2015 to around 114 deals in 2016, according to CB Insights.[17]

For all of the reasons that Dan and Saman had argued— training, motivation, and consistency of service—and also for the sake of avoiding lawsuits, switching from an "Uber for X" model to one that relied on employees had become a new trend in the gig economy.

Instacart, a startup that delivers groceries and once relied entirely on independent workers, also made the decision to hire workers rather than rely solely on independent contractors.

"This is something that people need to be trained on and coached on, on a regular basis," said Apoorva Mehta, the CEO.[18] Ultimately, Instacart offered training to employees that taught them skills like how to pick out a ripe avocado and the difference between basil and parsley. Shyp, a shipping service that initially relied on independent couriers to pick up packages from customers' homes and deliver them to its warehouse, made a similar change. In a blog post, Kevin Gibbon, the CEO, explained that moving to employees was "an investment in a longer-term relationship with our couriers, which we believe will ultimately create the best experience for our customers."[19] Delivery restaurants Munchery and Sprig also switched their couriers from independent contractors to employees shortly after launching. The gig economy remained prevalent, both in Silicon Valley and beyond, and some of the startups that switched away from using independent contractors failed even after hiring employees. But Managed by Q had to some extent proved the Good Jobs Strategy could work.

Running Managed by Q was still stressful, but a high rate of customers and cleaners quitting wasn't the reason. A growing source of tension came from a rift between the two cofounders.

Dan and Saman had once been co-CEOs, but now Dan was CEO and Saman was leading the product team. In the new office, they sat apart: Saman with the engineers, and Dan with the business team in a different area. Saman had moved out of New York City to Westchester after Q had launched, and if someone called at 3 a.m. because there weren't enough mops, it was usually Dan who dealt with the late-night emergency—a circumstance that sometimes grated on Dan when he was crawling out of bed in the wee hours of the morning to go shopping at Home Depot. The cofounders spoke less frequently and increasingly had different ideas about how the company should be run. "We started having disagreements [in the office] just like parents have disagreements in front of their kids," Saman said.

In January 2016, Saman left the company (he remains a major shareholder). "It's very much like being separated from your child," Saman told me more than a year later, describing the experience as "surreal." Though Dan felt the new arrangement was better for the company, he later described it as the hardest thing he'd ever done as CEO.

Managed by Q was still far from profitable, and the journey was not getting any easier.

PART IV

BACKLASH

CHAPTER 10

THE MEDIUM IS THE MOVEMENT

"UBER FOR X" STARTUPS QUICKLY BECAME SYNONYMOUS with the on-demand economy. Thanks to Uber's business model, city dwellers who were merely wealthy, and not disgustingly rich, could for the first time have every need filled at the push of a button. Startups would summon independent workers to deliver meals, shop for groceries, do laundry, or even park cars for just a small fee. "In the new world of on-demand everything," wrote one critic of this system, "you're either pampered, isolated royalty—or you're a 21st century servant."[1]

The price of this affordable royalty treatment was still falling. Under pressure to grow as quickly as possible, startups often discounted their services to attract customers and undercut competitors. Uber and Lyft engaged in a "price war" that would eventually in some cities make their services cheaper than public transportation. These price reductions were partially subsidized by venture capitalists who had invested billions in the companies, but they were also funded by cuts to drivers' pay. As Uber and Lyft became prevalent, the startups continued to cut fares and increase commissions, claiming a higher percentage of each fare as a fee. Customers, if they were aware of any impact that this had on drivers, didn't seem to care. Anonymized data from millions of credit card accounts showed that Uber's growth in weekly users started to accelerate in 2015.[2] By 2017, Uber had around 2 million drivers and 65 million customers worldwide, according to its cofounder Garrett Camp.[3]

Uber often argued that its drivers made more money when the company cut fares, and in certain supply-and-demand scenarios, this argument made sense. When Uber's prices dropped, more customers would use Uber, and there would be more work to go around. Meanwhile, as the low pay offered less incentive to drivers, some workers would drop out of the market, restricting the supply of rides and pushing the price back up.

In practice, this wasn't how it always played out. As Ethan Pollack, an economist who works with the Aspen Institute's "Future of Work" initiative, explained to me:

> While it's possible that lowering of per-trip
> payments would result in drivers receiving more
> money, it's unlikely, and if true would probably
> only be true in certain regions. So, for example,
> if drivers in a given region had a low utilization
> rate, and thus could be picking up a lot more
> passengers, then it's possible the increased
> volume would more than make up for the loss
> in compensation per trip. But if overall driver

compensation was going up, then this could tempt additional workers to start driving, thus lowering the volume a bit.

The point is, in order for overall driver compensation to increase when per-trip payments are lowered, there must be a very specific supply and demand situation, with a relatively flat supply curve (i.e. supply is unresponsive to price changes) but a steep demand curve (i.e. demand is very responsive to price changes). Even if that were true for some regions at certain times, it seems unlikely to be true for all regions at all times.[4]

What could be worse for drivers than the price cuts alone was that Uber's constantly shifting compensation model made it difficult for them to understand how much they would make the next day or the next week. "Imagine going into work one day and your boss tells you that you're going to have to do the exact same job you did last week but for 30% less money," wrote an Uber driver named Harry Campbell, who started a blog and podcast for ride-share drivers. "After a recent round of fare cuts, that is the exact situation drivers faced, and for many, this isn't the first time it's happened either."[5]

Some drivers looked for ways to protest these changes.

Abe, the Uber driver in Kansas City who had felt scammed by the company, was one of them. He decided that his Facebook page, Uber Freedom, which he'd named for the freedom

Uber provided through independence and flexibility, would stand for Freedom *from* Uber. "I have nothing to lose now," he said after being deactivated, hypothetically addressing Uber. "Let's go to war."

Abe wanted to start a union of sorts. Though he'd initially envisioned a group for Uber drivers in Kansas City, he almost immediately decided to take it to a national level. Abe parked his car at a gas station in his neighborhood and made a confessional-style video from the front seat that he headlined "UBER DRIVERS NATION WIDE STRIKE!!" He uploaded it to Facebook on October 3, 2015. "The time has come for all drivers across the nation to stand up to Uber and demand real change from Uber," Abe said in the video, before proposing a weekend strike. "We have to sacrifice a small window of time, just three days, for a greater future for all Uber drivers."

To make the video more visible, Abe bought a type of Facebook ad that promotes a post in people's news feeds. He watched the number of views climb, but it wasn't enough. Abe paid more. And then more. By the time he was done, he'd charged more than $4,000 to credit cards. The video had been viewed more than 250,000 times, and his page had an audience of 20,000 people who had "liked" it and would now receive its updates. "I spent boom, boom, money, money, boom, boom," he later recounted, sounding like a gambling addict. "I kept boosting. I kept seeing results. I kept doubling the budget, tripling the budget, quadrupling the budget."

Uber drivers, as independent contractors, couldn't join a

traditional union. But with this extra help from social media, what Abe imagined to be a different kind of labor movement for Uber drivers began. "It's going to be one of the biggest marketing campaigns that has ever been done to promote the strike," he told his new Facebook audience in another front-seat confessional video. "Hundreds of thousands, if not millions of people will be aware of the strike."

A list of demands for Uber followed:

1. RAISE RATES 60% NATIONWIDE

Uber was at the time cutting prices in an attempt to win over customers, which in turn lowered pay per mile for drivers. Abe's campaign requested it raise rates instead.

2. ADD TIP OPTION

Though tips were customary in the livery and taxi businesses, Uber discouraged them. "You don't need cash when you ride with Uber," the company explained on its website. "Once you arrive at your destination, your fare is automatically charged to your credit card on file—there's no need to tip." Many customers assumed that the tip was included in the fare, which in 2016 Uber would clarify, as part of a lawsuit settlement, was not the case.[6] Abe wanted Uber to go a step further and put an option to tip drivers in the app, as Uber's competitor Lyft had already done.

3. RAISE THE CANCELLATION FEE TO $7

If a passenger summoned an Uber driver but then canceled the ride after the driver was on his way, the customer usually paid a fee between $5 and $10, of which drivers could keep some percentage. In exchange for spending unpaid time traveling to a pickup point where a job never materialized, Abe wanted more compensation.

4. RAISE THE MIN FARE TO $7

Uber set a minimum fare for trips that spanned only a few blocks. After Uber's commission and fees, drivers sometimes only took home two or three dollars, which Abe felt wasn't enough.[7]

The plan, as Abe noted in another update a few days later, was also simple: "Phase one: Organize the biggest national Uber driver strike in Uber history, check! Phase two: get the main stream [*sic*] media involved and make the event go viral: in progress." Abe had written an official chant: "Uber's greed, puts drivers in need." It was great, he reasoned, because it was "very basic, very catchy, and it rhymes."

For an inexperienced organizer armed only with Facebook marketing tools and an overly optimistic outlook, Abe had generated by the end of October a surprising level of publicity. A local Kansas City television station covered plans for the strike shortly after Abe announced it, and small groups of drivers in the San Francisco Bay Area, Los Angeles, Seattle, and Washington, DC, had joined Facebook groups about local strikes and protests on the designated weekend.

When Abe arrived in San Francisco before the national strike, he was almost giddy. "This is really inspiring, for sure," he gushed in a video that showed one San Francisco organizer's black car, which had been turned into a poster promotion for the strike with white temporary paint. Abe was so excited that he couldn't eat.

That Friday morning at 10 a.m., he showed up at the office building that housed Uber's headquarters. A small group of drivers, many of them holding neon-colored poster boards with slogans written in black marker, stood in a semicircle around him as he spoke into a red-and-white megaphone. They didn't really know what to do, so they chanted, "Uber's greed, puts drivers in need!" In some videos of the protest, it looked as though there were more members of the media in attendance than drivers. "That might be true," Abe said, "but that's *more* of an impact, I think."

National news outlets like *Mashable* and the tech industry blog Recode covered the strike, as did local outlets in San Francisco, Washington, DC, Atlanta, Phoenix, and Detroit.

But even with media attention, the strike suffered from a logistical problem.

Unions first formed inside factories and mines, and on railroad tracks. Workers could find each other because they worked in the same place. Uber, on the other hand, didn't provide any way for "coworkers" to talk with each other. Online forums facilitated some communication, but a critical mass of drivers (who spoke different languages and used Uber in different ways) would need to proactively find the same Facebook group or forum to effectively coordinate action against the company. Even in cities where Uber drivers had organized strikes in the past, the majority of drivers had never even heard about them. "Unfortunately some drivers are out there working today," wrote one organizer on the Uber Drivers Network NYC Facebook page during a September strike, "NOT because they just want to cheat themselves and us, but because our message has not reached them YET."

Abe's solution to this problem was to drive around with a megaphone. One of his fellow protestors leaned out the back window announcing, in the tone and cadence that someone might use during a fire drill, "Do not use Uber. Use Lyft or Sidecar. Take a cab. Take the bus." Another video Abe posted in the Uber Freedom Facebook group showed a driver pulling up to another car. He rolled down his window.

"You work Uber?" the driver asked, in broken English.

The other driver confirmed that yes, he did.

"This weekend is a strike, you know? I work Uber too. This weekend, strike. Only Lyft, no Uber."

The other driver started to drive away, but the man filming the video kept yelling at him. "No Uber! Fuck Uber!"

At a victory dinner later that night, Abe watched himself on the local news. A few days later, the tech blog *Pando* published a story headlined "The Medium Is the Movement: Abe Husein Is a Labor Leader for Our Times."[8]

From the outside, Abe's strike looked like a genuine, grassroots effort to stand up to a giant company. But when I began interviewing Abe regularly, I quickly learned that his first priority was making money, not working toward social justice.

Abe was a jovial guy whose intense faith in his impending success was at times almost endearing. But he had personal philosophies that made him hard to like, such as a belief that racism didn't exist in America, that homeless people deserved no empathy, and that paying women to go on dates (a setup known as "sugar babies") was more respectful than trying to start a relationship. And aside from that, he lacked credibility. Lawsuits like the one he brought against Uber at the National Labor Relations Board were one of his favorite ways of rebelling against people with whom he disagreed. Abe loved lawsuits, he said, "because I don't have to pay anything." He was also suing a former employer, a restaurant business called Bravo Brio Restaurant Group, for non-tip-generating work he completed while waiting tables and bartending, jobs which could be paid lower than the minimum wage because tips were expected. After he filed the suit, he told me that he posted it in a company social network, where his managers would see it, and started taking conspicuous unauthorized breaks at the Panera next door. He wanted to get fired, which he said would help his case.

Even as Abe crusaded against the entrepreneurs who he believed had scammed him, he also obviously admired them. He had "researched the hell" out of Travis Kalanick and learned that Uber's CEO had taken some risks, like joining an early Napster-like startup that was later sued for billions of dollars for alleged copyright infringement. "He took a risk, and I respected that," Abe told me. "He kept going. It took balls to do that stuff." And even though Kevin Trudeau had scammed Abe out of thousands of dollars, Abe stuck to GIN's teachings about how to dress (for success), talk to people (with your hands), and win (believe). "It's telling you how to do life," Abe said. "Nobody teaches these things."

It seemed inevitable to Abe that by studying the tactics of these men, Kevin and Travis and others like them, he would achieve financial gains similar to theirs. Abe's favorite motivational CD was "Six Steps to Success" by Arnold Schwarzenegger, and he once repeated the headline advice to me: "Don't break the law, break the rules." He saw other successful people who had broken the rules, sometimes at his expense, and figured that was what success would take.

His belief in the "law of attraction" often led him to confidently pursue lofty ideas. These had in the past included running for Congress and would in the future include founding a company with the goal of putting Uber out of business. Launching a labor movement against Uber was just another big idea that fit into that pattern.

Talking about his strike, Abe concluded in a follow-up video, "Mission accomplished, for sure." But no, it wasn't "for sure." The media attention may have slightly annoyed Uber in the way a persistent fly might annoy an elephant, but it would be ridiculous to argue that the strike had impacted Uber's business. Driving around with a megaphone was not an effective method for informing other drivers about the strike, and the impact had clearly been limited. "A check of the Uber app on Saturday morning showed a number of available drivers for passengers," the local NBC affiliate in Washington, DC, had noted.[9]

Even in more traditional workplaces, strikes—once organized labor's biggest lever—have become so ineffective that they're now rare. In the 1950s, there were on average more than 300 strikes every year. In the 2000s, there were on average just 20 strikes per year.[10] What hope did a couple of guys with a megaphone really have?

Uber's professional public relations team managed to spin the publicity from Abe's protest into a pitch for the Uber job, using it as an opportunity to talk about "flexibility." In a sterile, almost comically off-topic response, it wrote to media organizations that covered the strike: "We always welcome feedback from driver-partners," adding about its gigs, "Drivers say they value the flexibility and the chance to be their own boss, and choose Uber over other options because it fits around their life and works for them." It was an impressive bit of jujitsu.[11]

Abe's resistance disintegrated quickly. Though he'd scheduled "Nationwide Uber driver strike round 2!" for New Year's Eve 2015 and, according to documentation in his Facebook accounts, paid an additional $6,500 to "boost" the announcement video, the protest hardly made a blip. And though he'd try to start a drivers' group with dues that would pay for marketing costs, when he showed me the administrator's view of his drivers' association website in July 2016, only 12 people had signed up.

Abe had also tried one other tactic to take revenge on Uber, which I didn't learn about until we spent several hours going through emails and accounts related to his organizing efforts. He showed me an email addressed to the Uber support staff on December 31, the day before his failed New Year's Eve strike. "I have an opportunity for you," it began. "If you give me 10k, I will take down my FB page and website and will not cause anymore uprising. I will disappear from the uber world. Or I can hand over admin access to you. This will be your one and only opportunity to make this movement go away." Uber did not take him up on the opportunity.

I was disappointed when I read the email, but after spending time talking with Abe, I wasn't altogether surprised.

Abe, it seemed to me, had felt powerless for most of his life. He'd first seen Uber as a way to take charge of his own destiny, be his own business, and maybe get rich while he was doing it. When that didn't pan out, he'd scrambled for any tactic that would help him gain control—protests, a lawsuit, a union, and even, I learned now, asking Uber to pay him to drop his organizing efforts.

There were plenty of driver-led efforts to protest fare cuts that hadn't involved asking Uber for a payment, though it's hard to identify one that got much traction. In the course of my time with Abe I also started talking with Mario Leadum, who was separately organizing drivers in San Francisco. He'd gotten off to a good start, organizing a large protest there, but eventually had given up.

Like Abe, Mario had joined Uber in 2013 after a friend told him he could make good money. At home, he had done the calculations. On $3,000 per week, which is what his friend told him was possible, he could buy a new car and still have plenty of money to make ends meet. So he quit his job in sales and marketing at an accounting firm, and he bought a Cadillac Escalade. Initially, he said, he could make about $3,000 in five long days.

Then Uber's fares started to drop, as they often did after Uber had established itself in a city. He started making $650 or $700 each week, driving the same hours. "It was greed," Mario said. "Obviously, it's all over the news, Uber is valued at $65 billion." Mario and a group of other drivers started meeting at the airport and near Candlestick Park in San Francisco to discuss their options. Less than a month after Uber announced another round of fare cuts throughout the country in January 2016,[12] he and other groups of drivers throughout the United States coordinated a protest.

The impact was bigger than Abe's version. The *New York Times* reported that hundreds of drivers gathered at the New York City Uber headquarters.[13] In San Francisco, Mario and other drivers led a caravan of honking drivers from Candlestick Park to City Hall and Uber headquarters. Michael Gumora, who runs a website called *Rideshare Report*, followed the caravan throughout all of its stops. "It looked like a sea of cars," he told *Wired*. "It looked like it spanned about two to three blocks of cars, four lanes across."[14] Enthused by their success, the drivers planned to disrupt Uber's business during the Super Bowl, which would take place in Uber's hometown of San Francisco.

The day of the game, police broke up a small gathering of

drivers near the stadium, but there was no disruption to Uber's service.[15] Uber had, according to Mario, guaranteed drivers $40 an hour during the hours around the Super Bowl. Mario planned another shot: "We have something else to respond to that," he said. "We are planning another event that is going to be really big. It's going to be seven times bigger than [the last protest]."

This event was set for February 26, 2016. Drivers began to organize not just along city lines, but among groups with which they shared culture and language. And all of these groups connected with each other. "We have the Ethiopian community, we have Arabic community, we have Brazilian," Mario said. "We have everything."

But February 26 came and went without news about a strike. Mario stopped returning my calls and text messages. Abdoul Diallo, who had been organizing drivers in New York, told me he'd decided not to participate in the February 26 protest. "Doing this for two years," he said, "you learn what works and does not work, and honestly, we've had very effective strikes in New York. But is it causing Uber to change its policies? Is it causing them to change what is harming us? And the truth is, it's not. We've seen them change things before, but then they find five other ways to still screw the drivers. They change one policy, they'll find five other ways to implement the same thing that is so-called changed."

Traditional unions had two options if they wanted to organize Uber drivers. The first was to argue that drivers were being treated as employees, and as employees, they could organize under federal collective bargaining laws. The second was to find some way outside of those laws to organize independent contractors.

A local chapter of the Teamsters in Seattle lobbied for a law that would allow Uber drivers to form a union. It passed. (Shortly later, the US Chamber of Commerce sued the city, saying the law conflicted with anti-trust law.) In Germany, a group of workers' organizations created a list of best practices that, as of 2017, eight crowdsourcing companies had pledged to follow. Together they established an office where workers could report violations of this code.[16]

Regardless of the strategy, long-established unions faced the same problem as novice organizers like Abe, which was that they didn't know who worked for gig economy companies. The International Association of Machinists and Aerospace Workers union in New York City solved this problem by striking a deal with Uber in which Uber officials agreed to hand over contact information for its New York City drivers. This enabled the union to form an "Independent Drivers' Guild" through which drivers could appeal Uber's decisions to deactivate them.

But the reaction of the labor movement to this announcement was anything but unified. In its partnership with Uber, the union agreed to forgo challenges to Uber's classification of those drivers as independent contractors. The not-quite-union Drivers' Guild would still not bargain over a contract, which wasn't surprising, as independent contractors working together to set prices for their services could be considered collusion. While some saw Uber's agreement with the Guild as a step in the right direction, others saw it as a public relations effort that protected Uber rather than its drivers. New York Taxi Workers Alliance executive director Bhairavi Desai called it a "historic betrayal" and promptly filed a lawsuit with ten Uber drivers that accused Uber of misclassifying workers as independent contractors.[17] Abdoul Diallo, the Uber driver who helped organize other drivers in New York, said the Drivers' Guild sounded "bogus,"[18] and he encouraged drivers to instead sign cards that would allow the Amalgamated Transit Union to represent them.

As unions searched for the best approach to organizing Uber's drivers, Uber noted it was making improvements to its gig. In the summer of 2016, the company promoted a partnership with the online radio service Pandora as a benefit to workers. The new deal allowed Uber drivers to use the premium version of Pandora for free. Another feature allowed drivers to pause ride requests when they wanted to take a lunch break, instead of simply denying a request (which might eventually lead to being deactivated from the platform if it happened too often), and another paid drivers for waiting to pick up a passenger for longer than two minutes. Needless to say, these efforts seemed shallow.

At that point, Uber still hadn't added a tipping feature to its apps, though nearly every group of organized drivers had requested one. Tips don't necessarily make their recipients better off, but they are standard in the livery and taxi businesses, and it would have been easy for Uber to add the option to its customer app. Uber had always resisted because it wanted transactions to be one step easier for its customers. "Riders tell us that one of the things they like most about Uber is that it's hassle-free," the company wrote in a 2016 blog post. "And that's how we intend to keep it."

Uber didn't give in on tipping until it faced a public relations crisis in 2017. Susan Fowler, a former employee at the company, published a blog post that documented a culture of sexual harassment and misogyny at the company, which led to an internal investigation that ultimately resulted in the firing of 20 employees and the ousting of Travis Kalanick, who resigned amid a shareholder revolt. The company was so desperate to mitigate the impact of this news that on a steamy summer day in New York City, it plopped a giant block of ice near Union Square, inside of which were "collectable cones" that could be taken to McDonald's for ice cream (Uber had in previous years delivered free ice cream in the summer, but this was a truly over-the-top display). Nearby, Uber staff distributed happy-toned pastel shirts to random people on the street.

Around the same time as this summer branding campaign, Uber declared a commitment to "180 days of change" in which it would improve its experience for drivers—in addition to a new tipping option, it added extra payments for drivers who traveled a long distance to pick up a rider (previously time that went unpaid) and notifications that told drivers, before they agreed to accept a ride, when the trip would take longer than 45 minutes (which meant they could avoid ending up in the middle of nowhere, with a long return trip they would have to make on their own dime).

These improvements still fell far short of what some drivers had demanded. But the distributed nature and independent status of Uber's workforce made it difficult to organize, and aside from the PR crisis that made the company desperate to improve its image, Uber had little business reason to give drivers more control over their micro-businesses or to honor their other requests. Uber's service simply moved people from point A to point B, and it wasn't clear that drivers could provide a meaningfully better service if they were happier with Uber. Nor was it clear that customers would pay more for it. As long as Uber could find as many drivers as it needed (which was easier in a down economy), the company didn't have a financial incentive to make the driver experience a huge priority.

An executive who Uber unsuccessfully tried to recruit in 2016 told *The Guardian* that during his job interview, Uber's chief product officer had responded to a question about how the company would handle the discontent among its drivers by saying, "Well, we're just going to replace them all with robots" (an Uber spokesman told the paper that its executive did not recall making the statement).[19]

On her applications to universities, Kristy had described her Mechanical Turk work as a "crowdsourcing micro-contractor" position, a job that she noted included working with several Fortune 500 companies. She hoped to study psychology.

Mechanical Turk had shown Kristy how close many jobs were to being automated. She'd been part of a crowd that helped train machines to do things like recognize images and diagnose diseases, and she knew that someday those algorithms wouldn't need training anymore. They'd replace the humans currently doing the work. As far as she could tell, though, people would always want a therapist to offer a real human connection.

With her husband back at work, Kristy had been able to save the money she earned from Mechanical Turk for her $10,000 annual tuition. She hoped that a degree would finally lead to work that would allow her to save for retirement.

Kristy started classes at Ryerson University in 2012. Most of her classmates were in their early twenties, and she sometimes feared she was the weird old person in the class, the one who sat in the front row and always raised her hand. Sometimes she participated in her classmates' Facebook groups, using an anonymous account she had set up for the purpose of entering contests. In person, she had a more difficult time making friends with them.

Though Kristy had stopped working on Mechanical Turk full-time when she started school, she had continued working as the moderator of Turker Nation. The forum kept her in contact with her fellow Turkers, her friends. It also sparked her interest in activism.

On the forum, she'd connected with academic researchers who were interested in Mechanical Turk work. Some, like Stanford's Michael Bernstein, studied how crowd work might be applied to bigger and more complicated problems in the future. Others, like Six Silberman and Lilly Irani, who had built a tool used by Mechanical Turk workers to rate and review clients, studied what the emergence of crowd work might mean for workers. Kristy agreed to speak with a group of these researchers when they visited Toronto for a conference.

They met over dinner at Kristy's favorite Indian restaurant. And as they discussed Mechanical Turk, it wasn't long before Oscar Smith came up. "Smith" (probably a pseudonym) used Mechanical Turk to transcribe thousands and thousands of business cards. He was, according to Kristy, notorious for bad pay—he only offered a penny per card—and Mechanical Turk workers suspected he worked at a professional social networking site that, at the time, offered a service in which customers could take photos of business cards in order to automatically add them to their contacts. The casual discussion turned to what Turkers could do to convince Oscar Smith to raise his pay.

Everyone at the table well knew that it would not be easy to organize Mechanical Turk workers in such an effort. Some were hesitant to challenge Amazon's policies, if for no other reason than Amazon could easily shut the whole site down. In its annual report, which documented $136 billion in net sales, Amazon didn't even mention its crowd work platform. The company was known for rapidly launching and closing new businesses—grocery delivery, home cleaning, a Pinterest-like shopping platform—and one imagined it would have few qualms about shuttering Mechanical Turk. Any attempt at collective action would need to be managed carefully. It would also be made difficult by the fact that Mechanical Turk workers were distributed all over the world, spoke many languages, and had significantly different ideas about how many dollars translated to a living wage. Traditional unions wouldn't work.

But maybe there were other forms of collective action that would. What if workers could hold bad employers' work hostage, as a "strike" of sorts? They'd sign up to do the job, but not actually do the work. After the allotted time expired, when the tasks would be released back to the platform, another member of the resistance could pick up the same work and continue to hold it. Because they hadn't actually completed the work, Oscar Smith would not have a chance to reject that work, and therefore could not impact their ability to get other work in the future.

Or maybe Mechanical Turk workers could accept all of Oscar Smith's tasks, but do the work in a slightly wrong way. The phone number would be off by one digit. The address would have the wrong zip code. Oscar Smith might not notice in time to leave the Mechanical Turk worker a bad rating. His customers would.

Though the conversation had started as a hypothetical exercise, the researchers and Kristy alike started to see potential in some of these ideas. Sabotaging Oscar Smith's work might be too extreme, but the strategy of collective action made sense.

Kristy agreed to keep in touch with the people she referred to as "the academics." She asked for feedback on the ideas from other Turkers (not all were pleased, fearing retribution from Amazon) and eventually helped researchers launch a website called Dynamo. Lilly Irani, Michael Bernstein, and Niloufar Salehi, a Stanford graduate student, led the project along with two other Stanford students and Kristy, who was an author on the eventual paper.

Dynamo was designed to help Mechanical Turk workers plan a movement. Here's how it worked: Its creators posted a task on Mechanical Turk that was open to anyone who had completed 100 jobs or more. In it, the researchers explained that they were paying the Turkers for a five-minute-long vacation. Turkers could decide either to do nothing, and still collect their pay, or to visit Dynamo and sign up with a code provided. This served a dual purpose of recruitment and screening—only active Mechanical Turk workers would have the code—without violating workers' desire to be anonymous (which was legitimate, as union laws would not protect them if Amazon decided to kick them off of Mechanical Turk in response to their participation).

Inside Dynamo, anyone could start a "campaign" by writing a description of it. Members could vote ideas up or down, and when an idea collected at least 25 positive votes, then it would be moved to a project space with tools for outlining action steps and tracking progress. The site launched in 2014.

Around the same time, Kristy got invited to her first big public speaking event. She had emailed a Microsoft researcher after reading about her work with crowdsourcing platforms (Kristy emailed anyone she read about who seemed interesting), and that researcher had introduced her to a Pittsburgh conference organizer. When she was first asked to speak, she didn't really know what to say. So she set her session up as an interview, with Michael Bernstein asking her questions about Mechanical Turk.

It was the first time she'd been to Pittsburgh, and she wasn't sure how she'd react to speaking to a large group of people, many of whom had doctoral degrees. But as she started to talk about her experiences as a worker on Mechanical Turk, she realized that she was actually enjoying herself.

"Oh my god," she thought. "I'm good at this. And I'm not scared at all."

Six months in, Dynamo had 470 registered users. Of 22 proposed ideas, two had made it to the point of action.[20] Dynamo's first campaign created a set of ethical guidelines designed to curb bad behavior by academic researchers, who used the site as a cheap way to recruit research participants (by 2015, more than 1,120 academic studies on Google Scholar would include Mechanical Turk workers as participants).[21] Despite Mechanical Turk's growing popularity as a research tool, study ethics boards did not always hold these experiments and surveys to the same standards as research conducted in person.

In one example that particularly irked Kristy, a graduate student at the University of Washington had devised a study in which he recruited Turkers to tag photos without disclosing that they were part of a study. Unsuspecting Turkers who signed up were first met with nice pictures of animals, much like the ones I had spent hours tagging in my own Mechanical

Turk experiment. Then, sometimes, the photos grew more gruesome. One Turker wrote on Turkopticon, a tool that Mechanical Turk workers use to share reviews of task posters, that the photos were "90% pretty cute kittens, rays of sunshine, cupcakes and brownies" and the other 10% were "the polar opposite—dismembered children in the streets, burn victims, amputations, decaying corpses, etc." The graduate student and his fellow University of Washington researchers wrote a paper based on the research and in a draft explained that they were testing "differences in labor supplied depending on the 'agreeableness' or 'disagreeableness.'" They'd found images for the study by searching Google Images for topics such as "amputations, autopsy, broken limbs, gangrene, and larvas to name a few."[22]

Though some Turkers said they didn't really mind being used as lab rats, just so long as the job paid, other workers believed that studies like this one wouldn't exist if study ethics boards (like the institutional review board that approved the disagreeable image experiment) were better informed. Throughout the first six months of the ethical guidelines campaign, 171 workers and 45 task requesters signed the formal, academically worded guidelines.[23]

The list of signatures begins, thanks to Dynamo's pseudonymous nature and automatically generated usernames (which uses the convention "adjective + animal), like this:

Gorgeous monarch butterfly (14 August 2014)
Courageous cockroach (14 August 2014)

Fancy cod (15 August 2014)

Faithful fly (15 August 2014)

Dark bird of paradise (15 August 2014)

Elated sea urchin (15 August 2014)

Lonely wombat (15 August 2014)

Amused hedgehog (15 August 2014)

Jolly otter (16 August 2014)

Terrible cat (16 August 2014)

It was not the most authoritative list of names, no, but it was something.

Kristy proposed the second Dynamo campaign. Her biggest concern was that employers on the platform sometimes did not treat workers like humans, partly because Amazon's description of the service didn't frame them that way or acknowledge their individual existence. Amazon's slogan for Mechanical Turk is "Artificial artificial intelligence." The Mechanical Turk website homepage used a simple flowchart graphic to explain to new workers how the gig worked: Find an interesting task-> Work-> Earn Money. "Work" was represented with an image of wheels turning, rather than by a human worker. Unlike other gig economy platforms, employers never saw the name of the people who worked for them through Mechanical Turk. "When you have something that is not humanized, like your refrigerator, you have no empathy for it," Kristy said. "You don't care if you slam the door. You don't care if you leave moldy food in it. It doesn't matter. You don't care about the refrigerator."

Her solution to being treated as less than human by clients

on Mechanical Turk was simple: Ask Turkers to explain the problem in letters to Jeff Bezos, the CEO of Amazon. The bullet points on Kristy's campaign memo, below a "WHAT WE WANT TO SAY" headline, read as follows:

1: Turkers are human beings, not algorithms, and should be marketed accordingly.
2: Turkers should not be sold as cheap labour, but instead skilled, flexible labour which needs to be respected.
3: Turkers need to have a method of representing themselves to Requesters [people who hire Mechanical Turk workers] and the world via Amazon.

Kristy's own letter was heartfelt and polite. It made a business case for treating workers better, not unlike the case that Dan and Saman had once put together for Managed by Q.

Dear Mr. Bezos,
I am a Turker: middle age, entrepreneur, university student, mom, wife, reliant on my mTurk income to keep my family safe from foreclosure. I don't Turk for $1.45 per hour nor do I live in a developing country, I am a skilled and intelligent worker, and I Turk as my main source of income and it is currently my chosen career. I am a human being, not an algorithm, and yet Requesters seem to think I am there just to serve their bidding. They do not respect myself and my fellow

Turkers with a fair wage, and in fact say that we should be thankful we get anything near to minimum wage for the "easy" work we do. Searching for work all day isn't easy. Having to find and install scripts to become more efficient isn't easy. Dealing with unfair rejections isn't easy. Being a Turker isn't easy.

I ask that you look towards not selling us as cheap labour, but instead as highly skilled labourers who offer an efficient way to get work done. Paying each of us less than fairly isn't the way to save money, but instead using a huge workforce available at any hour of the day is what will reduce costs. Please stop selling us as nothing more than an algorithm and instead introduce those who use your service to the fact we are living, breathing beings who are using this money not to buy beer, but to feed, clothe and shelter our families. If you could facilitate our communication with Requesters somehow, be it through a forum or just presenting our stories to them, I think it would change their perception of us for the better. Remember: the more that they pay us, the more fees you make. The better they treat us, the better the results they get, and the more likely they are to stick around. The better mTurk's reputation, the more new Requesters will use the service. When Turkers are happy, Requesters are happy, and Amazon will be happy, too.

Thanks for reading,
Kristy Milland

Amazon did not publicly acknowledge the letter campaign. It did not change its branding of Mechanical Turk. It did not create a minimum wage or a new worker rating system. Nor did it create a system in which workers could better communicate with Amazon.

However, *The Guardian*, *The Atlantic*, *Fast Company Magazine*, and *Wired* all covered the campaign. "The goals of the campaign, which hopes to eventually beam hundreds of letters into Jeff Bezos's inbox, are as varied as the Turkers themselves," wrote *The Guardian*. "Some just want to celebrate Mechanical Turk's flexibility and bite-size tasks. Others are demanding a more modern website that allows them to market themselves to employers and, in return, rate companies as good or bad to work for."[24]

Amazon responded to at least one letter, in which a Turker in India had written to say that his paper checks often got lost in the mail.[25] Soon after, the company enabled bank transfers to India. When I talked with Kristy in early 2015, she was optimistic about the implications of this small victory and the media attention.

"I think workers know now that they can work toward change," she said, "and the word is out that we're human beings. So now, the question is, how else do we get ourselves to be more visible? What do workers want? And how do we mobilize them to try new campaigns?" She wanted to keep the momentum going. "We built a foundation that shows, yep, we could absolutely get together and do things," she said. "What's next?"

After finishing her degree in psychology within four years, Kristy decided to get her master's in labor studies. She had started calling herself an activist and speaking at events all around the world: at Carnegie Mellon, at the Foundation for European Progressive Studies, to the Group of the Progressive Alliance of Socialists & Democrats in the European Parliament. She spoke in Berlin, Brussels, and Rome.

While speaking in Brussels, Kristy learned that the Swedish white-collar trade union Unionen had started to incorporate freelancers. That gave her faith in unions as a model for organizing non-traditional workers. Her faith in Dynamo, though, didn't last.

In 2016, almost two years after Kristy started the Amazon Mechanical Turk letter-writing campaign, I checked in with her again. While Dynamo had added 470 users in its first six months, in the last year and a half it had only added about 75. The most recent campaign idea had been posted seven months earlier by one of the researchers who built the site.

The researchers who started Dynamo had moved on to other projects, and nobody had the time to keep it alive. The latest project to have achieved 25 votes aimed to create a badge academic task posters could use on their profiles as a signal that they followed the Dynamo ethical guidelines. But according to Kristy, nobody ever volunteered to actually design it.

Amazon, meanwhile, had effectively hampered Dynamo by interfering with its sign-up process. In winter 2015, it removed the Mechanical Turk tasks that Dynamo had used to distribute sign-up codes, saying that they violated the terms of service by "requiring registration at another website or group." No federal laws protect collective organizing in the gig economy. And whether it was this interference from Amazon or the lack of manpower that had led to Dynamo's demise, Kristy had by then lost her belief in virtual organizing as an effective lever for change. Dynamo at that point looked more like a ghost town than the future of labor organizing.[26]

CHAPTER 11

UBER FOR POLITICS

POLITICIANS NOTICED THE GIG ECONOMY AND ITS PROMISE to shape the future of work sometime around 2015.

That September, I met Mark Warner, the senior US senator from Virginia, in New York City, at one of those hole-in-the-wall delis that serve coffee in Styrofoam cups. Warner, a tall man, conservatively dressed in a dark suit, was seated so close to a cooler that he had to move his stainless steel chair every time someone wanted to buy an orange juice.

The senator was as well positioned as anyone in Congress to understand the changes wrought by the gig economy. Before becoming a politician, he'd been a venture capitalist, making a fortune by investing in early wireless phone businesses. A Democrat who shared his party's concerns for working people's rights and wages, he was also the third wealthiest man in Congress. He'd positioned himself as both pro-business and pro-workers, and he'd gotten in touch with me after I'd written an article about how the realities of working in the gig economy didn't live up to the pitch.

Over the last several months, Senator Warner and his staff had met with gig economy executives from a range of companies including Lyft, Postmates, and Handy. He'd also been host-ing round-table conversations with gig economy workers in Virginia. "Eight or nine months into this," he told me, "I'm more sure than ever that this is a fundamental shift in the economy and is going to accelerate."

In 2015, only about 0.5% of all US workers had participated in Silicon Valley's labor revolution.[1] (In the UK, the percentage was higher: The Chartered Institute of Personnel and Develop-ment estimated in 2017 that 4% of all UK workers have par-ticipated in the gig economy.[2]) Warner knew that the startup world's version of the gig economy was still, in the context of the wider economy, only as big as a rounding error. It was so small that companies often wondered out loud why journalists, and now politicians, worried so much about its impact. But he didn't really have much sympathy for that argument. "You can't have it both ways," he argued. "You can't say, 'give me this valuation as I'm pitching this world transformation,' and then say, 'why are policy makers interested?' When Airbnb has more rooms than Marriott, and Uber has 250,000 drivers and dramatically disrupts a market, it will attract attention."

The gig economy's outsized influence and growth trajec-tory were one reason Mark Warner had to be interested in this small subset of startups. The second was that the gig economy made a perfect vehicle for talking about a problem that stretched beyond Silicon Valley. At the heart of it was a new status quo throughout the United States and much of the world: Risk had migrated from companies to workers.

This was true of those who had watched their employment

opportunities, over decades, become increasingly fractured into a web of contractors, freelancers, temps, and other non-traditional employment. It was also true of employees with full-time jobs, who, unlike gig workers, were covered under all labor protection laws but had still seen the holes in their safety nets widen. Evidence of what the political scientist Jacob Hacker had called "The Great Risk Shift" in his 2006 book of the same title was everywhere.

- Pension plans had all but died. Between 1983 and 2013, the percentage of Americans covered by the benefit had slid from 62% to 17%.[3] Instead, employers were offering 401(k) plans for retirement savings,[4] because a typical 3% match to an employee's contribution is less expensive than the 7% to 8% of payroll it takes to fund a pension program.[5] If the market doesn't perform in this arrangement, it's the worker, not the employer, who takes the hit. Even the 401(k) plan was mostly a perk for the wealthy: 89% of private industry workers in the Bureau of Labor Statistics' highest wage category had access to retirement benefits, compared to 32% of workers in the lowest wage category. A startling number of people—30% of the civilian population—*had no retirement savings or pension.*[6]
- Unemployment insurance had thinned at the same time as retirement benefits. In December 2014, only 23.1% of unemployed Americans received

unemployment benefits from state programs—an
all-time low that replaced the previous record set
at 25% in September 1984.[7] Federal emergency
unemployment benefits, which provided extensions
after state benefits ran out, expired at the end of 2013.

• And then there was health insurance, often a more
immediate concern. Gig economy workers in the
United States had no legal claim to the benefit at all,
unless they qualified for government programs
designed for the especially young, old, or poor.
Among US workers who relied on sites like Mechanical
Turk for their primary income, almost 40% didn't
have health insurance.[8] But even employees whose
employers did provide health insurance were taking
on more of the cost. Between 2005 and 2015, worker
contributions to employer-sponsored plans on average
increased 83%.[9] The average amount workers paid
almost doubled, outpacing growth in workers'
earnings and overall inflation.[10] Only 24% of workers
in the bottom quartile of wages participated in an
employer-sponsored plan.[11] President Obama's
Affordable Care Act established a marketplace for
buying insurance and aimed to make doing so easier
for self-employed people; during the first year it was
fully in place, the number of uninsured Americans
dropped by 25%. But the plan was flawed in important
ways, one of which was that politicians promised to
dismantle rather than repair it.[12]

All of these trends—deteriorating retirement savings programs, weakening support for unemployed workers, and declining health benefits—have over decades compounded into
unprecedented insecurity for everyone, not just those in the gig
economy.

Household income in the United States became noticeably
more volatile between the early 1970s and the late 2000s,[13] and
a Federal Reserve study published in 2014 found that a third
of American households experience volatile income swings,
mostly due to unpredictable hours.[14] In 2004, when the *Los
Angeles Times* reported the results of a survey that followed
5,000 families for 40 years, it concluded that "a growing number of families have found themselves caught on a financial
roller coaster ride, with their annual incomes taking increasingly wild leaps and plunges."[15] The paper compared the new
economy to the stock market, with an unpredictable schedule
of big payouts and big setbacks for workers.

This was a theme park ride that few people enjoyed.

Labor leader David Rolf and venture capitalist Nick
Hanauer, writing in the journal *Democracy*, explained why:

> Economic security is what frees us from the fear that
> one job loss, one illness—one economic downturn amidst
> a business cycle guaranteed to produce economic
> downturns—could cost us our home, our car, our family,
> and our social status. It's what grants us permission to
> invest in ourselves and in our children, and to purchase
> the non-subsistence goods and experiences that make

our lives healthier, happier, and more fulfilling. It gives us the confidence to live our lives with the realistic expectation of a more prosperous and stable economic future, and to take the entrepreneurial risks that are the lifeblood of a vibrant market economy. A secure middle class is the cause of growth, not its effect; in fact, our economy cannot reach its full potential without it. And a middle class that lives in constant fear of falling out of the middle class isn't truly middle class at all.[16]

"If our captains of industry are so certain that certainty is necessary for industry," Rolf and Hanauer concluded, citing a common argument against changing business regulations and adding new benefit programs, "then it surely must be true that their customer base, the American middle class, needs some of that certainty as well. For without the certainty that they will remain in the middle class, middle-class Americans simply cannot fulfill their crucial economic role."

Just as the gig economy is an extreme version of the economy-wide trend away from direct employment, so too—with its total lack of safety net benefits—was it an extreme version of the increasing insecurity felt by even the directly employed portion of the middle class.

Throughout my years reporting on the gig economy, I bumped into this insecurity constantly. I found it when I interviewed Kristen Logan, who lives in Merced, California, and had with the help of Samaschool found a gig doing customer service for a beauty school in New York. She loved the gig, but said "it is scary because at any point they could decide there's not going to be a school anymore, and then I'm back to square one." I found it when I talked with Sarah, an Uber driver in Boston, who had rented a car to work in the gig economy and shortly later damaged it in an accident. Between car insurance payments, repair bills, and time off from driving, which was how she had planned to make money, she wasn't sure if she would be able to recover financially. I found it in Abe's dream of being a millionaire. Why did he care so much about becoming rich that he valued it above everything else? When I'd asked him, he had seemed confused about my curiosity.

"Are you a rich person?" he responded earnestly.

I'm not poor by any stretch, but I'm a journalist. "No," I told him.

"There are three different realities," he told me, with an absoluteness that made me feel like he was about to quote from a GIN teaching, which he was. "There's the reality of poor people. The reality of middle-class people. And the reality of rich people. When you're rich, you can do things nobody else can do. You're truly free. If you and I lose our jobs, we'll be done in a matter of months. For most people, it's a matter of days."

Few people would put it exactly like this, but the numbers actually back Abe up. According to a report from the Federal Reserve released in May 2015, 47% of Americans could not cover an unexpected $400 expense with their savings or credit card.[17] There's no cushion between those people and a total free fall.

Back in the New York deli, Senator Warner explained that

he wanted to campaign for some compromise, recognizing that there would be trade-offs in any policy. "You don't want to squash innovation with top-down policy too early," he said, launching into what would become his stump speech. "At the same time, you don't want people to operate on a high wire with nothing in between." Gig economy companies had told him that, according to their surveys, what workers really wanted was more cash, not benefits.[18] "I understand that," Warner said, "but nobody wants disability until they hurt their hands and you're a jewelry maker."

With the support of gig economy companies like Postmates, DoorDash, and Lyft, Warner eventually sponsored a bill that, if signed into law, would fund $20 million worth of experiments around benefits better suited for non-traditional workers. "The social contract was set up on the idea of you're going to go work for one firm for 30 years, and you've got all these benefits for doing that," he told me in an interview when he announced the bill. "That's not the case anymore. We can bemoan the fact that's not the case forever, or we can say, let's create a system that will work for the world today."[19]

Talking about the app-based gig economy—a Silicon Valley creation that impacted a minuscule percentage of the workforce—was a way to talk about big issues such as instability, insecurity, healthcare, and retirement savings. The difference was that talking about the gig economy attracted attention.

Uber, the most visible gig economy company, was one of

the most exciting business stories of the decade. What had
started as an idea inspired by two friends' trouble getting a cab
(on "a snowy Paris evening," no less, according to the company's official account), had grown within years into a global
empire—an astounding feat. Uber's cofounder and longtime
CEO, Travis Kalanick, meanwhile, had an interesting story
line of his own. Often portrayed as a belligerent frat boy, he
seemed hell-bent on ruthlessly eliminating any obstacles to his
company's success, whether they be rivals like Lyft (whom he
reportedly tried to sabotage with thousands of fake ride requests), local regulators (whom he "mowed down" in New
York, as per a headline in the *Washington Post*), or global competition (this one didn't work out so well, as Uber eventually
ceded its China business to a formerly competitive partner). The
Uber story was so entertaining that Universal and 20th Century
Fox both announced Uber-themed movies during the same
week (as of this writing, Universal and 20th Century Fox plan
to make zero movies about retirement security).

Headlines about Uber were much more attractive than
headlines about important government decisions, and Mark
Warner was not the only politician who had figured this out.
As the gig economy gained momentum, Democrats and Republicans alike used it as a way to frame conversations about
larger, less-exciting issues.

In the first economic policy speech for her 2016 presiden-
tial campaign, Hillary Clinton talked about Americans who
"are making extra money renting out a spare room, designing
websites, selling products they design themselves at home, or

even driving their own car," later adding the Democratic party line on worker classification issues—that she would "crack down on bosses who exploit employees by misclassifying them as contractors or even steal their wages."[20]

Republican candidate Jeb Bush, eager to demonstrate his support for business and innovation, simply tweeted a photo of himself in an Uber.

Democratic senator Elizabeth Warren, long a proponent of strengthening the government-provided safety net, finally won headlines for the position after pairing it with the gig economy. "The much-touted virtues of flexibility, independence and creativity offered by gig work might be true for some workers under some conditions," she said in a speech at an annual conference for the New America Foundation in Washington, "but for many, the gig economy is simply the next step in a losing effort to build some economic security in a world where all the benefits are floating to the top 10 percent."[21]

The speech wasn't exactly about the gig economy: "The problems facing gig workers are much like the problems facing millions of other workers," Warren noted. But the headlines were definitely about the gig economy: "Elizabeth Warren Takes on Uber, Lyft and the 'Gig Economy'";[22] "Elizabeth Warren Calls for Increased Regulations on Uber, Lyft, and the 'Gig Economy'";[23] "Elizabeth Warren Slams Uber and Lyft."[24] In her speech, Warren had acknowledged that talking about TaskRabbit, Uber, and Lyft was "very hip." It seemed she was right.

Sometimes politicians and labor leaders didn't even need to

frame their positions within the context of the gig economy to have them interpreted that way. The media did it for them. When the Labor Department's Wage and Hour Division published new guidance on worker classification in July 2015 (which would later be rescinded by the Trump administration), it did not mention Uber. Invariably, mainstream media coverage of the memo did.[25] Never mind that, as a US senator in 2007, President Obama had introduced legislation that proposed closing a loophole employers used to classify their employees as contractors. Or that David Weil—who had dedicated the most recent portion of his career to studying the breakdown of the employee-employer relationship outside of Silicon Valley—was now the administrator of the Wage and Hour Division. This was about Uber.

The Economic Policy Institute (EPI) had written briefs about the need for changes in policy around the contingent workforce as far back as 1991. Now it framed these themes in the context of the gig economy.[26] "The really big picture is, this is part of a trend in the declining labor share of the economy," EPI president Lawrence Mishel told me. Was it frustrating that the first time I'd called him was to talk about Uber? Probably. Mishel also bylined an exasperated op-ed for *The Atlantic* in which he argued that "dwelling on these companies too much distracts from the central features of work in America that should be prominent in the public discussion."[27] Another way to look at all this dwelling on Uber's business model, however, was as a tool for making these very central features of work more prominent.

By October 2015, the debate around the gig economy had gained enough momentum that President Obama made it a topic of discussion at a White House summit of union leaders, economists, and employers. Perched on a wooden stool during a question-and-answer session, the president noted the gig economy's wider significance: "The on-demand economy or the share economy is still a fraction of the overall economy," he said, but "someone in the on-demand economy is just one end of this broader spectrum of changes that are taking place across the board. We need to make sure workers across sectors understand that their fates are connected. They can't think, 'Ok, I'm in a union in a factory with a traditional contracted pension, and so I don't have to worry about what is happening to that worker over there.' Because the same problems that they're dealing with, you may eventually be dealing with."[28]

As with anything related to changes wrought by the tech sector, the "future of work" panel circuit boomed. ("I want to start a conference about the 'present of work,'" joked Managed by Q's Dan Teran, who made frequent appearances.) Moderators wanted to know: As the full-time job became less standard, how should our policies change? How could workers be heard in a company that did not claim them as employees? Could the idea of a good job transfer to a good gig?

The gig economy helped reinvigorate a conversation about security that had been ongoing for decades. Labor organizers in both nontraditional and traditional workers' advocacy groups contributed new ideas about what collective action could look like in the new world of work and how benefits should be arranged. Politicians made cautious statements about how the dissolution of the direct employment relationship should impact policies.

Harder to spot than the endless panels were the small actions that these types of conversations produced. But they were there, if barely: The Freelancers Union had been campaigning since 2011 for the federal government to reinstate its survey of the contingent workforce, which it had abandoned after budget cuts in 2005. Obama's secretary of labor, Thomas Perez, finally promised to do so, noting that "the on-demand economy raises important questions about how to continue upholding time-honored labor standards and how to promote economic security for American workers in a changing labor market."[29] (The department conducted the survey in May 2017.)

An unlikely group of collaborators, meanwhile, came together to advocate for the same type of benefits that Warner would propose in his bill. The collective included business executives at companies like Lyft, Etsy, Instacart, and Handy; academics; venture capitalists; the leader of a Service Employees International Union (SEIU) branch; and representatives from untraditional organized labor like the National Domestic Workers Alliance and the Freelancers Union. In November 2015, it produced an open letter in support of "portable benefits."

Portable benefits are social insurance programs that aren't tied to an employer but rather move with workers from job to job. In the United States, Social Security is one example of a portable benefit. Multiple employers pay into a worker's fund, and when the worker moves jobs, they don't lose the benefit. Healthcare, paid sick days, and other social insurance could, the letter proposed, work in a similar way. Though the letter was short on details, the broad coalition vaulted the phrase "portable benefits" into the *Wall Street Journal*, *New York Times*, and *Washington Post*.

When Phyllis C. Borzi, Obama's assistant secretary for the Employee Benefits Security Administration, US Department of Labor, spoke at the Aspen Institute months after the White House summit at which Obama had spoken, she commented on the change. "There's been a lot of focus on retirement benefits and security, primarily because of the focus on the on-demand economy," she said. "And that's a good thing, that we're focusing on this, because it's possible that with a new set of characters and a new impetus to look at this issue, we might be able to actually get something done."[30]

Restructuring benefits was one of the ideas for mitigating the insecurity inherent in the gig economy. The other was to restructure employment categories.

Former deputy secretary of labor Seth Harris and Princeton economist Alan Krueger summarized the case for a new category of "independent workers" in a December 2015 policy paper for the center-left Washington think tank the Brookings Institute. Gig economy relationships with workers, they argued, don't look like traditional contractor relationships. Uber drivers and Handy cleaners accept whatever rates and terms of service the company sets. But workers in the gig economy also choose when to work, and work for multiple companies at the same time. "Their relationships with intermediaries are not so dependent, deep, extensive, or long lasting," Harris and Krueger wrote, "that we should ask these intermediaries to assume responsibility for all aspects of independent workers' economic security."[31]

Their solution was one that other countries had already adopted: a third employment category between employees and independent contractors. As they envisioned it, this third category of workers would allow gig economy companies to purchase and administer certain benefits for workers without worrying about providing evidence of misclassification. It would also give companies the choice to opt in to payments for some types of protection programs, like workers' compensation insurance.

Inherent in proposals like this one was the idea that the work gig economy companies provided was valuable and worth protecting. And to some workers, companies like Uber really did provide a safety net of sorts. As one driver, former *San Francisco Chronicle* journalist John Koopman, explained: "When you're falling straight down the financial cliff face, you reach out to grab hold of anything available to stop your descent and there, just before you land in a homeless shelter or move in with your sister, is Uber. I think of Uber as a modern-day version of the Works Progress Administration during the Depression. Thanks to Uber, I am not poor. I am just . . . nobody."[32]

A new "independent worker" category offered something

to all parties involved. Companies like Uber would not need to totally revamp their business models, because they wouldn't commit to the full cost and liability of hiring employees, and their workers would have more rights and protections. The authors of the Brookings Institute report even got a little poetic about it, asking readers to imagine a tent: "With only the two poles, the middle of the tent will flap sloppily in any reasonably strong wind. But the introduction of a third pole to hold up the middle of the tent will reduce the flapping and give more shape to the tent, even if the tent is not perfectly taut."[33]

Union leaders were not moved by the metaphor. "The AFL-CIO Executive Council affirmed that working people in the gig economy share a single common designation: employees," the largest federation of unions in the United States wrote on its blog four months after the Harris and Krueger paper was published.[34] Above an excerpt of the statement on its website, the union posted a graph with three lines over time. One showed productivity, angling up and to the right. The other two represented average hourly compensation as estimated in two different ways, with both lines leveling off around 2005. There was no attempt to link the image to the text of the statement, but the point was clear: Companies are getting richer, and workers aren't. The AFL-CIO believed a third category of workers would enable, not hurt, this trend.

In countries that have introduced a third category of workers, the addition hasn't ended the conflict between wanting to control workers and wanting to classify them in a more independent, less expensive category. In London, for instance, the question of how to classify Uber and Deliveroo workers has been hotly debated. When an employment tribunal in 2016 ruled that Uber's drivers were not self-employed, as they'd been classified by the company, but were "workers" entitled to holiday pay, paid rest breaks, and the national minimum wage (Uber appealed the decision), the trade unions leader Frances O'Grady told the BBC: "For many workers the gig economy is a rigged economy, where bosses can get out of paying the minimum wage and providing basics like paid holidays and rest breaks . . . We need the government to get tough on sham self-employment."[35] It was not so different from arguments that gig economy detractors have made in the United States, where no third category of workers exists.[36]

Critics of the UK's in-between worker category, as well as similar categories in Italy, Spain, and Canada, often argue that these classifications just intensify the problem: that with another option between employees and independent contractors, employers find more loopholes for opting out of the laws and benefits associated with traditional employment. Still, the idea of creating a new type of employment category in the United States gained some support.

Handy's political PR firm eventually helped draft state legislation that combined a version of this idea with portable benefits. According to a draft Handy circulated for discussion in 2016, companies under the proposed law could elect to contribute a portion of each transaction to an on-demand worker's benefit fund—which he or she could put toward benefits like life insurance and dental care—and, as a result, be certain the workers would remain independent contractors. The independent contractor classification would apply to even work done previously for the company, essentially removing Handy's risk of misclassification lawsuits.

Hiring employees can cost 20% to 30% more than hiring independent contractors. Social Security and Medicare payments alone cost 7.65% of a worker's pay. By comparison, Handy had proposed companies divert at least 2.5% of worker pay into a worker benefit account. Those who opposed the plan worried that it would look to some on-demand companies like a bargain; that it would allow them to classify workers as independent contractors (albeit, independent contractors who had access to small benefits funds) when they would be more properly categorized as employees, who have more rights and protections.

Others who signed on to the idea of "portable benefits," the same term Handy used, had very different ideas about what they would look like. David Rolf, a vice president of the SEIU, writing with venture capitalist Nick Hanauer in *Democracy*, laid out his specific plan: "Mandatory accrued benefits should include a minimum of five days a year of paid sick leave, 15 days a year of paid vacation leave, a matching 401(k) contribution, and the same health insurance premium contribution as currently required under the Affordable Care Act (ideally, healthcare would fall into the insurance benefit category, but that is a larger battle)."[37]

In this version, contributing to independent contractors' benefits would not be a choice. Benefits would accrue to all workers regardless of classification. If someone worked 20 hours for one employer, that employer would pay half of the benefits to which someone with a 40-hour full-time job would be entitled. Other employers for whom that person worked would pay into the same account.

Further disagreement existed even among people who shared this vision. Who would handle these accounts? Employers? Third-party startups? Non-profit organizations? Some argued that this could be the role of unions in the twenty-first century. The Screen Actors Guild, for instance, had a benefits fund for actors who typically work on project-based gigs with multiple employers. The only problem with using the same system in the gig economy was that the law that enables this type of account, called Taft-Hartley, only applies to traditional unions. You can't set up a Taft-Hartley plan if you're not a union. And you can't form a union with independent contractors. "All we have to do is create a classification of provider that could operate outside of Taft-Hartley," Rolf told me.

Few of the debates around additional worker classifications or portable benefits resulted in concrete outcomes. Two years after Harris and Krueger proposed a third category of workers in the United States, the idea had largely faded from discussions about the future of work. Two years after Handy circulated a draft of the New York state bill, it still had not made it to the legislative docket. Other attempts at starting portable benefits programs had proven just as slow. Senator Warner's proposed $20 million fund for portable benefits pilot programs hadn't yet made it out of committee. A small $100,000 grant program for experiments with portable retirement benefits savings plans introduced by the Department of Labor[38] had given awards to three projects, but only one was even in the prototype stage of its exploration (the other two used the grants to conduct research on the barriers that low-wage workers faced in saving for retirement).

On panels about the future of work, nearly everyone could agree that the current social safety net and worker classification systems were no longer adequate. But actually implementing changes—which would require parties with different political agendas to compromise on specifics, experiments that proved feasibility, and passage through a slow law-making process— was more likely to take decades than years.

PART V

THE FUTURE OF WORK

CHAPTER 12

PIVOT

IN THE SPRING OF 2016, MANAGED BY Q LEASED A NEW office in a New York City skyscraper. The company had grown from 150 to 500 employees in the last year, and its previous home in the East Village, in a five-story building with a rickety elevator that featured exposed brick walls, could no longer accommodate enough desks. This new office by comparison looked like a huge corporate office. Or, at least, it would once the company moved in.

Eventually Managed by Q would install glass walls to create conference rooms, purchase desks and chairs, and strategically place plants to add a pop of color throughout its new office. It would install a receptionist desk formed in the shape of a "Q." But on March 18, the day of the startup's first formal press conference, no furniture or walls had yet been installed, and the floor was still unfinished. Managed by Q was working from a temporary space on another floor. Its permanent office looked as though someone had moved the basement 11 stories into the air—it was a vast cement cave, empty except for a catering table filled with coffee and croissants, several rows of folding chairs, and a podium.

Dan Teran nervously approached the microphone, flanked on one side by Ty Lane, one of Managed by Q's first operators, and on the other by Thomas Perez, the secretary of labor of the United States. Standing behind the rows of seated reporters were his friends, including his cofounder, Saman.

Saman had started a new company shortly after leaving Managed by Q. But he was proud of what he and Dan had started, and he found it astonishing that what had begun as two guys thinking about residential buildings in Park Slope and Williamsburg had so quickly turned into a large company with a mission that interested the secretary of labor.

Dan began his speech: "When we were just starting out a few years ago . . . We looked at the tech companies around us that were increasingly looking at labor as a cost and not an asset . . ." As he spoke, he lightly tapped his foot on the floor. A handful of reporters tapped on their laptops. "As the secretary will tell you, that's what leads to bad jobs, stagnant wages, and unmotivated workers. It's bad for workers. It's bad for customers. And it's bad for business. So we took a different path. Instead of shirking our responsibility as an employer, we [leaned into it]. In order to provide the best service, we need the best people for the job. And in order to attract the best people for the job, we need to be the best employer. So that's what we set out to do, and that's what we're after today."

Companies in other sectors, like Starbucks and the burger restaurant Shake Shack, had programs that offered equity to ground-level workers. Managed by Q, Dan announced, had decided to bring the idea to tech startups by designating 5% of its equity shares as stock options for field operators like Ty.

It was a milestone moment. Starting any company is difficult. Dan sometimes looked sleep deprived, and he rarely took a day off. His personal relationships suffered under the weight of his work commitments, and he went through hard periods when people quit or had to be fired. Because Managed by Q had taken on the task of defining a good job, there was another difficulty on top of those shared by most entrepreneurs. Dan had to figure out policies that could work both for software engineers and for cleaners who were paid by the hour, and he had to at least try to understand the challenges faced by a workforce with whom he had little in common.

Even after all of this effort, the result was quite humble. It was hard work scrubbing toilets and desks for fair wages and basic security. Managed by Q had figured out how to make it good for business by selling other office services and supplies, and by reducing the number of customers who quit its service and the number of workers who quit its jobs. In a better world, the concept wouldn't warrant a press conference. Still, Managed by Q had created a little bit of the impact Dan had once been looking for when he wanted to be a politician.

As Secretary Perez took the microphone from Dan, he addressed the Managed by Q workers in the audience. "When someone asks you 'Where do you work? What do you do? What are you building?'" he said, "Tell them, 'You are building the middle class in America, that is what you're doing.'"

•   •   •

The next day, Managed by Q had plans to explain its new policies at an "operator assembly," one of the regular gatherings
that had evolved from Managed by Q's early pizza parties with
its subcontracted cleaners. All employees at the company
gathered for food, updates, training, and awards.

The meeting felt more like a family reunion than a stodgy
press conference. Black-and-white streamers weaved between
pipes on the ceiling. Toddlers roamed around with their parents, and a buffet of pulled pork sandwiches had been set up
next to a stack of paper plates and a cooler full of soda. Instead
of the sounds of reporters' keyboards and Dan's foot nervously
tapping on the floor, soda cans popped and conversations broke
into laughter.

Dan, though, looked like he was on the verge of tears.

"I'm sure you noticed on your way in," he told me, "that
there's a union asking people to sign cards."

Managed by Q was no longer quite part of the "gig economy," because it had made a decision to hire employees. And
employees, unlike independent contractors, had the legal right
to form a union. A local branch of the United Construction
Trades and Industrial Employees Union—which was small
enough that it listed administrators' first names on its voicemail greeting—now hoped the workers would choose to do so.

If its employees were to unionize, Managed by Q's business
would need to change. The startup typically didn't compete

with the unionized companies that cleaned high-rise buildings, but rather with those that cleaned smaller office buildings that, unlike many New York City skyscrapers, had no obligation to use only unionized workers. Dan feared he wouldn't be able to compete against those smaller companies' prices if he were to both comply with the union's prevailing wage and offer his current benefits package (for a worker who opted into every benefit, he estimated the hourly cost of that package to be around $20 per hour).

I felt conflicted by Dan's nervousness at the union's appearance. A union official conceded that Managed by Q's wages weren't particularly bad—that "it wasn't treating workers like dogs"—but said the startup was still "nowhere near where it needed to be." And it was true that Managed by Q's starting hourly wage was significantly lower than that for unionized cleaners who worked in high rises.

But by this point I had observed Managed by Q for more than a year, interviewing both executives and workers, and I had seen how it consistently made decisions that improved jobs, even when under no requirement to do so. It had gone so far as to offer workers fully paid healthcare benefits and equity, both uncommon in janitorial work (and professional work, for that matter). Its workers spoke highly of the opportunity to advance along a career path. Wasn't this, too, a valid model for creating good jobs?

Even if Dan were worried about the union organizers that were hovering near the office building door, as he started speaking into a microphone, he looked more comfortable than he had at the formal press conference. "I know it's Saturday," he started, "but personally there's nowhere I'd rather be." He ran through the highlights of the past few days, how the secretary of labor had come to speak at Q, and showed photos of "these beautiful operators" whose well-lit portraits had appeared in the *New York Times Magazine*.

Again, he spoke about how the business benefited by providing good jobs as he ran through the new benefits. Managed by Q would start contributing to workers' 401(k)s, so that every time they put in a dollar, the company would match it with another 50 cents.

"How many folks here have kids?" Dan asked.

Most of the room raised hands.

"I don't. I have a dog."

More laughter.

Managed by Q would begin paying up to 12 weeks of full salary for operators after the birth or adoption of a child. The benefit would be based on tenure and whether the employee was a primary caregiver, but Managed by Q would contribute to fathers' incomes while they spent time with new children, too.

"Now the last thing, that I'm probably most excited to share with you guys," Dan said. "Everybody here knows that Q is a startup, right? We've all seen in the papers that the guy who painted the wall at Facebook made millions of dollars because he was paid in stock. Well, I'm here to tell you today that this isn't a place where only the executives and software engineers are going to do well if we build something big. Over the next five years, we'll be giving away five percent of the company to the operators working in the field."

Most startups don't survive long enough to be acquired or go public, and the ultimate value of the gesture might be nothing. Juno, a startup ride-hailing service that had promoted itself as a good employer, had also offered workers equity. It had recruited independent drivers under the premise that it offered them better terms, but had under-delivered on its promises when a competitor bought the company for $200 million. Advertising materials for Juno suggested that Juno's equity units were worth $0.20 per share, but in the end, they were worth as little as $0.02 per share, leaving drivers with only pocket change.[1]

Dan hoped that, if nothing else, the gesture of offering equity shares would convey a message. "This is incredibly important for me to communicate to you," he said. "It's not my company, it's not the company of the people who work in this office. It's every single person here's, we are all on the same team."

After his speech, the group split up to attend smaller sessions focused on training, on answering questions about the new benefits, and, in one room, on just getting to know each other. But before they dispersed, Dan referenced the union. "I think you guys who have been here for a while understand that we're deeply, deeply interested in building this company together," he said, "and I think that our operators are exactly the right people to represent themselves."

Operators cheered just as hard as they had for their new equity packages. "Yeah, Dan," someone screamed. I passed Dan on my way out. "After that, I feel much better," he said, once again looking like he might cry.

About a year later, the union submitted a petition to the National Labor Relations Board to represent Managed by Q's workforce, but on the day of a scheduled hearing, it withdrew the petition because it hadn't collected enough votes from workers.

In October 2017, Managed by Q announced that its cleaning and handyman operation was not only a direct employer of around 700 workers (about half of them full-time), but a profitable business. The Good Jobs Strategy had not yet created a blockbuster hit startup, but it had survived.

In 2014, Trebor Scholz, a professor at the New School in New York City, left a conference panel about "the future of work," as he put it to me, "with the words of a Mechanical Turk worker ringing in my ears." The panel had discussed how little voice workers felt they had in their employment conditions on the platform. When they faced problems like clients who "rejected" their work, saying they were unsatisfied and wouldn't pay (but who still kept and used the work for free), there was no way to challenge the decision. Similarly, they had no systematic way to request features that might make their work easier to complete or to report abusive clients.

"If all these critiques [of Mechanical Turk] are true,"

Trebor remembers the worker saying, "then why don't we build our own platform?"

The worker was Kristy.

After the disappointment of Dynamo, the online organizing platform for Mechanical Turk workers Kristy had helped build, she had come to the conclusion that the only way to make sure the interests of crowd workers were considered was to have workers run the platform. To bring an old idea— cooperatives—into the new economy.

Trebor agreed. It was an idea around which he eventually based a book and a conference that was attended by 1,500 people.[2] He named it "platform cooperativism."

Typical arguments against cooperatives are that they are slow—voting on decisions takes time—and that they lack the means to market themselves. But, Kristy and Trebor both argued, technology could solve some of these problems. Voting could take place electronically, which would make it faster. Marketing theoretically would be cheaper using social media and digital advertising. The digital infrastructure for a ride-hailing app or a task marketplace, unlike a brick-and-mortar building, could be shared between several different companies. And the emerging blockchain technology, the decentralized ledger-keeping system behind the success of Bitcoin, promises to make transactions between people easier and less costly by making them incredibly secure and transparent without intermediaries.

Still, Trebor was often asked: Could a self-funded cooperative really compete with venture-backed startups like Uber?

The lobby of Uber's San Francisco headquarters featured a ceiling-high world map outlined on a black wall, with blue dots sprinkled over most of it, to show where Uber's service was available. They sure had a head start.

That's not the point, Trebor believed. "These questions are coming from the assumption about profit maximization rather than serving a set of members," he told me in an interview. "You don't need to destroy Uber. But can you create an ethical, smaller alternative?" In other words, if you're not trying to create a jackpot win for investors, there's really no need to paint a black map on the wall with which to track an expanding empire. All you're trying to do is provide work for the people who own the company.

For obvious reasons, when workers have more control over company direction, they fare better. What may be less intuitive is that giving power to workers also arguably benefits companies. In German-style "codetermination," for instance, workers take seats on company boards and form "work councils" that address day-to-day issues. While many once argued that Germany wouldn't be able to sustain this system in a globalized world, a report from the Brookings Institute recently pointed out that, in fact, codetermination has shielded Germany from the detrimental impacts of short-term fixes to create shareholder value.[3] As Susan Holmberg, the report's author, explained in a *Quartz* op-ed:

Executive stock options, which incentivize irresponsible risk taking [and] fraud . . . are viewed by the German public and its workers as highly suspect, and they are issued at a much lower rate than in the United States. And while German executive pay has risen, it is nowhere near the levels of America's juiced up executive pay, which has become a major driver of our inequality crisis. In 2015, the typical German CEO made $5.6 million while their U.S. counterparts took home $14.9 million. Beyond the numbers, the German sense of executive strategy and purpose remains intact.[4]

Platform cooperatives would take this concept to its logical extreme. They would be the ultimate expression of worker voice.

Starting a cooperative business, like any business, comes with some unique challenges. When in 2016 I interviewed Joshua Danielson, the cofounder of a cooperative version of Task-Rabbit called Loconomics, he had just started to recruit the first service providers after more than a year of working on cooperative bylaws. Getting to that point had taken more time than expected. "We thought we'd go global within a couple of months," he said. "Easier said than done."

Joshua didn't have the resources to hire a team, and he had been willing to go into debt for the cause. "I'm a 37-year-old white male with an MBA," he said. "I'll be fine no matter what happens."

The plan was that workers on Loconomics would pay $30

per month to belong to the cooperative (eventual fees, depend-ing on the type of membership, varied between $0 and $39 per month). All of the money they earned would be theirs—Loconomics wouldn't take a cut—and at the end of the year, the dividends would be distributed back to the workers. "When you have people performing services for you that aren't having 20% to 40% of their pay taken away," Joshua said, "they're probably going to do a better job. Hopefully we'll attract people who want to create their own business, create their own brand."

Stocksy, a cooperatively owned stock photo site, had been able to make this theory work. Together its 900 members cre-ated $7.9 million of revenue in 2015, more than half of which was paid out to them in royalties (the site pays much higher than industry average). Stocksy paid a $200,000 dividend to its workers that year, just two years after it was founded by an iStockphoto cofounder and an iStockphoto early employee. "We realized we could do it differently this time," one of Stocksy's founders told the *New York Times*, which noted that photos on Stocksy "are far from the standard fare found on many stock photography sites" in that "colorful portraits, un-expected compositions and playful shots greet visitors."[5]

Kristy imagined she'd build a cooperative platform for crowd workers as part of her Ph.D., which she hoped to com-plete after finishing her psychology undergraduate degree. "Picture it like the internet," she told me in 2015. "There is a central node. It will be the node that creates the software, pro-vides the information and the payment processing. There will be a search function, like Google in a way, where you can search workers." Each worker would also have a personal platform that employers could access directly, and be able to set his or her own rate. Employers could either handpick individuals to hire, if they were looking for a skilled worker, or they could fill out a template to hire an entire crowd, say, if they wanted to categorize a database of 10,000 images. Each person would have an identity—not just a number—and the ability to form relationships with employers.

Trebor frequently discussed efforts such as Kristy's planned platform. "If contingency is the new reality," he and a coauthor Nathan Schneider wrote in an essay for *Fast Company*, "how can we turn it into a good thing? We can't expect the depressing trend of platform labor to change unless we demand and create a different way of doing business."[6]

Terrence knew funding for the Samaschool Arkansas program was running out, and he could tell that the program hadn't been making a scaleable impact, despite its good intentions. The non-profit had most recently tried to use its model for work centers in East Africa and India in Dumas—its sales team pitched companies to win work that it then hired the program participants to complete—but it was hard to find projects that paid an Arkansas living wage. So Terrence wasn't at all surprised when Samasource's managing director broke the news to him, in a phone call, that the organization had decided to leave Dumas altogether.

Terrence may not have been entirely surprised, but he was a little angry. He was angry that most of his students, due to circumstances beyond their control, didn't have the resources to participate on digital platforms. They didn't have the computers, they didn't have the internet speeds, and they didn't have the right skills.

A few months later, I met Terrence at a McDonald's in Pine Bluff, Arkansas, a city of about 45,000 people where he now lived.

"Hey, how are you doing?" he asked a kid in a white tank top and gym shorts as he ran past our booth. He was one of Terrence's neighbors. As the boy, who looked about ten years old, told us he was doing ok and bolted into the bathroom, a woman at another table yelled after him, "Where are your shoes?"

The boy appeared again a few minutes later. "What did you eat today?" Terrence asked him. He could use a burger, he muttered, and Terrence got up to order one.

"You can say, let's go to Arkansas and get people jobs," Terrence said. "That's a great ambition. It's nice to talk about and write about. But then you start to think about what it takes." If Silicon Valley really wanted to make a difference in Dumas, Terrence believed, it needed to study the people first. When it did, it would realize that digital apps, or a couple of grants, couldn't make an impact on poverty that had been gaining momentum for more than a hundred years. That programs like Samaschool needed ten times as many resources to be effective.

The presence of the digital gig economy wasn't enough to solve the problems in Dumas. In non-US cities like Nairobi, Samasource was able to hire its workers and provide them with benefits and support. It was able to hire managers to help with coaching and quality control. In the United States, the gig work on which Samaschool focused meant going without even the basic security that you'd be paid a wage commensurate with the hours you worked. For most of Terrence's students, this wasn't anywhere near enough support. They had problems more pressing than spending time searching online platforms for work.

In Desha County, where Dumas is located, 27.8% of the population is food insecure, compared to the national average of 13.4%.[7] According to a final report Samasource wrote about its Dumas program, 44% of Terrence's students throughout the three years of the program did not have reliable transportation. And around 15% of Samaschool's Arkansas participants had faced some type of homelessness while taking Terrence's class. Terrence provided transportation when his students needed it, wrote letters to courts in an attempt to keep them out of jail for small violations, and counseled them when they were having trouble paying their water bills. He brought pizza and snacks to class. But one man and a ten-week course wasn't enough to hold together the lives of 30 students at a time.

After Samaschool realized that it wasn't able to provide the level of intervention required to support residents in Dumas, the non-profit changed its program completely. Now, instead of teaching its own classes, the non-profit partners with workforce development programs around the country—many of which provide training in marketable skills—to teach their students and clients how to access independent work involving those skills. It gave up on the idea that these students would compete in a global marketplace and instead focused on in-person gigs like carpentry, housecleaning, babysitting, and delivery.

Connecting skilled workers with the gig economy provided the possibility that they could use their gigs to build their resumes or tide themselves over with freelance gigs while they looked for other jobs. "The typical workforce development organization that provides training for job seekers is really focused on full-time jobs, and it relies on employers to provide onboarding and training and support," Lindsey Crumbaugh, the program's managing director, said. "What we're saying is we need to reframe the whole way that we train to build the skill of being a problem solver, a micro-entrepreneur, so individuals have the ability to move between full-time and independent work, because a lot of trends we're seeing [indicate that] forms of independent work will be a lot more prevalent."

Gig work wouldn't necessarily solve the problems of poverty, and it didn't come with the safety net protections of employment. But increasingly it was the work that was available. And there was a new set of skills required to access it, skills like self-promotion and entrepreneurship. In its new role as a partner to other organizations, Samaschool would continue to focus on these skills.

In terms of efforts toward helping his own community went, Terrence was back to his habit of asking children if they were hungry.

He'd been thinking deeply about why Samaschool hadn't worked, and what might have worked better. A policy idea called "Universal Basic Income" (UBI) had started gaining steam in Silicon Valley as a way to end poverty. Programs based on this idea pay everyone a minimum income, regardless of their circumstances.

Martin Luther King Jr., the conservative economist Friedrich Hayek, and President Richard Nixon had all supported this idea, and modern boosters were no less varied. They included Andy Stern, the former president of the SEIU; the libertarian economist Charles Murray; and Robert Reich, the Bill Clinton–era labor secretary, who was fond of comparing the gig economy to a sweatshop. The tech incubator Y Combinator had recently committed to running a UBI experiment in California to understand how it worked. Facebook cofounder Chris Hughes endorsed UBI in a book.

Terrence Davenport, though, was not a fan. He was nearly exasperated at what he saw as the ignorance inherent in the idea. "Do you know about the opioid crisis in this country?" he said. "Do you know that poor people in my community don't know how to budget?" He told me that he felt Silicon Valley was a place full of "the leaders of our country" who don't know anything about it.

At the time, the other most prevalent idea for ensuring Americans better income came from Donald Trump, who had campaigned for the presidency on an "America First" ideology, which implied that sending immigrants home would help Americans get jobs. This, too, seemed ridiculous to Terrence. The African Americans he knew didn't have the skills for the jobs currently filled by immigrants, he told me. Any actual solution needed to account for the inherited trauma and hopelessness experienced by the people in Dumas. Training wasn't enough. There are plumbing apprenticeships in Little Rock, Terrence explained. Those are good jobs, they pay well. But if someone in Dumas enrolled, they would still need transportation, they would need child care, and they would need a place to stay. Which is why, if Terrence were to start an organization, he'd give everyone a case worker. They wouldn't need to have a behavioral problem or commit a crime to get support. Being chronically unemployed was enough of a condition. He'd call the operation "H.U.G.," Helping You Grow.

Terrence's brush with Silicon Valley had also inspired him to think more about the resources in Arkansas. About the land that stretched for miles outside of Dumas; about the state's agriculture industry, which was one of the top producers in the country; and about the Tyson feed mill, part of a $28 billion food company, located just miles from where we were sitting.

It seemed to Terrence that the community wasn't using these resources in a way that benefited the majority of its residents. And he'd started to see opportunities where it could correct this everywhere, even in Dumpsters. Terrence had attended a city council meeting in which a $14,000 decision was made to purchase Dumpsters. He'd remembered how, after his mother died, when he had moved back to Dumas and was looking for work, he dug up scrap metal to sell by the pound. Why not teach Dumas residents to weld? he thought. Teach them a skill, give them a gig, and probably wind up with cheaper Dumpsters as a result?

Silicon Valley didn't need to fix Dumas's problems. Dumas could do it. If its leaders learned to think differently about how to use its resources, they could make a gig economy of their own. "If you hadn't eaten for three days, and I put a piece of bread in front of you," Terrence told me, setting down a hypothetical slice on the McDonald's table between us, "and then I say, watch this bread, and I leave, you will eat the bread and we'll put you in jail. But I could have given you a piece of bread as payment for watching it." His point was that instead of putting people in jail for the types of crimes that they were likely to commit if they couldn't otherwise meet their basic needs, it was possible for the community to put them to work in a way that would both help them meet those needs and also benefit others.

The gig economy had early on been positioned as an easy way to solve hard economic problems like unemployment and unequal opportunity. And in this regard, it had plenty of competition. Get-rich-quick schemes like GIN, the one Abe had fallen for, promise their followers easy success. Bestselling self-help books like *The Secret* and *You Are a Badass* trumpet the same idea, that one can manifest anything by believing in it. Multi-level marketing companies tell women they can become successful entrepreneurs by selling makeup, candles, or essential oils (though almost nobody in the "triangle-shaped" organizations—it's not a pyramid, they all insist—makes money doing so).

The solutions Terrence proposed were of a completely different tone than those that I heard from startups. They weren't simple. They were resource-intensive and multi-dimensional and individual.

Terrence knew better than most people working at technology companies that in reality, we don't all have the same chance of succeeding if we just believe. What entrepreneurs most have in common is not a special leadership style, flavor of grit, or talent. It is inheritance or other access to startup capital, according to a study published in the *Journal of Labor Economics*.[8]

Those at the top of the economic ladder had built-in advantages, and moving up the ladder was only getting more difficult. In a 2016 study, University of Massachusetts economists used data from the US Census Bureau to show that social mobility in the United States is decreasing.[9] "The probability of ending where you start has gone up, and the probability of moving up from where you start has gone down," one of the researchers told *The Atlantic*. Someone who started in the middle of the earning distribution in 1993 was 20% less likely to reach the top two earning deciles within the next 15 years than someone who started in 1981.[10]

Problems like insecurity and inequality are complex and slow to fix. Just believing cannot solve them. A book or a special club cannot solve them. And, in the case of the gig economy, neither can an app. The more Terrence thought about it, the more he became convinced that truly making a difference in Dumas would be slow, difficult, and definitely not on-demand.

CHAPTER 13

A VERY SERIOUS ISSUE

ON A HOT DAY IN MAY 2017, ENTREPRENEURS FROM ALL over the world, including Managed by Q's Dan Teran, packed themselves into a warehouse event space just off of New York City's FDR Highway for TechCrunch Disrupt. Half trade show, half *Shark Tank*–style pitch competition, Disrupt is a tri-annual startup conference where startups with names such as Happification, Binary Mango, and Blazesoft come to get noticed by venture capitalists and the tech writers whose blogs they read. As an attendee, it's hard to walk anywhere without acquiring a free branded T-shirt.

Dan wasn't there to pitch Managed by Q—he was there to participate in a keynote talk with the CEO of Handy, Oisin Hanrahan. The two entrepreneurs had taken very different approaches to their cleaning and handyman services. Dan's version served offices and relied on employees. Handy's customers were households and its cleaners and handymen were classified as independent contractors.

Despite these completely different approaches, it was hard to say from a business perspective which company had turned out to be more successful. Managed by Q was at that point a mid-size company with 3,000 clients, and on the brink of profitability. Handy as of November 2016 operated in more than 28 cities and had raised more than $110 million of venture capital. Though the latter startup's early struggles in maintaining both customers and workers had been well documented, they hadn't been a death sentence. *Inc.* magazine had recently profiled Handy's "painful path to profitability."[1]

At TechCrunch Disrupt, the stage was cordoned off from the rest of the conference by thick black curtains, but the buzz of optimistic entrepreneurs was still so loud that the audience strained to hear the on-stage conversation. Dan and Oisin would be interviewed by a third man, *TechCrunch* editor Jon Shieber. Both speakers wore blazers, dress shirts, and jeans—Dan's were black, Oisin's were denim—and, at first, they looked like teenagers forced to mingle at a dance. Which, since TechCrunch didn't tell them they'd be appearing together until announcing it publicly, wasn't so far off the mark.

"Is the gig up for this business model?" Jon began. "Is it all over? Has the song been sung? Has the sun set?"

It was a fair question. Many of the companies that once called themselves part of the gig economy, with exceptions like Uber, Lyft, and Handy, had either changed their business models or failed. And as the economy had recovered—six years of continuous US job growth and counting—it seemed that fewer people were willing to take their jobs piecemeal, from an app.[2] Participation in gig economy platforms had been falling since June 2014, according to data from the JPMorgan Chase Institute. More than half of the people who started working in the gig economy quit within a year.[3]

At the same time that workers were dropping out of the gig economy, legal issues were making the business model look riskier. There had always occasionally been scary court rulings, like the one in California that determined a single Uber driver was an employee. But court cases take years to wind their way through the system, and everyone with meaningful funds to devote to the situation (companies that want to avoid a massive disruption to their business models, lawyers who want to be paid) had an incentive to settle rather than risk losing a case. Uber settled a pair of its most threatening misclassification lawsuits in California and Massachusetts by agreeing to pay drivers $100 million (an arrangement later declared inadequate by a judge), and Lyft, which had previously tried to settle a class action suit in California for $12.25 million, eventually agreed to a $27 million payment to drivers. Nobody wants to lose millions of dollars, but in the context of what colloquially was known as these companies' "war chests" of funding, the settlements didn't meaningfully impact their businesses.

Recent rulings looked more threatening. In 2017, New York's state labor department upheld a court decision that had determined that three former Uber drivers, as well as "similarly situated" drivers, should be treated as employees for unemployment insurance purposes. And in the UK, the Transport for London would soon strip Uber of its license, saying it was not a "fit and proper" private car company. Shortly after that, a tribunal would reject the company's appeal to a ruling that found its drivers were not self-employed, entitling drivers to paid time off and a minimum wage. (In each case, Uber continued with the appeals process.) During the same stretch of bad news for Uber, the top EU court dealt the company a major blow when it ruled that it should be regulated as a taxi company rather than a technology company that merely connects drivers and riders.

The gig economy, as Silicon Valley had invented it, had largely come and gone. It had not, however, ceased to be relevant.

Long before the gig economy, large companies outside of Silicon Valley had started moving away from direct employment relationships. Startups like Uber demonstrated new strategies and technologies that could make this process more efficient. They broke work into parcels, automatically coordinated workers, and established practices for using apps as management. These were all developments that non-startups would emulate.

Julie Sweet, the North America leader of Accenture, a professional services company with clients in 120 countries and 40 industries, told me in June 2016 that she imagined soon there would be a company that only hires c-suite executives. "The ability to outsource corporate functions is high," she said. "For my main workforce, I can tap into the gig economy." (She did not foresee this shift for Accenture itself, which she said is "built on relationships" and "not a transaction industry.") Gigster, the startup that routed jobs to Curtis after he'd quit his job in New York City, had all but achieved this. By 2016, it had

32 employees—only four of whom helped manage its 500 client projects. Everything else was accomplished by automation and freelancers. Stephane Kasriel, the CEO of Upwork, similarly saw the world shifting to non-employees as an inevitability. "We have freelancers who manage ten people, we have freelancers who access secure code databases, we have freelancers who have been working with us for 10 years," he told me during a meeting in June 2015. "As long as the legal status is clear, there is no difference."

Before he left, his PR handler gave me a printed Power-Point presentation that compared the gig economy to ecommerce. "Commerce has moved online and now services, including work, are too," one of the smooth color-copied slides beamed. A graph showing freelancer earnings jutted straight up and to the right, pausing at $3.2 billion at the end of 2014. On the last slide, the presentation urged me to imagine what this meant for the future. "Commerce, still a small percentage of retail, is a huge market," it said. "Imagine if only 2% of work moves online."

The impact of this shift might be a good thing for professional workers with in-demand skills. But the trend wouldn't necessarily stop with these workers. IKEA bought TaskRabbit in 2017, presumably so it can dispatch workers to assemble customers' furniture. Amazon started rolling out a courier program in 2015 that offers the opportunity for workers to be their own boss and work on their own schedules delivering Amazon packages. And a new round of startups hopes to bring more corporations into the gig economy.

Take Wonolo, an on-demand staffing agency built on Uber's model. It works with more than 600 businesses, including Papa John's, Johnson & Johnson, and Target, to provide on-demand labor. Wonolo workers fill in when businesses need extra help but don't need to hire full-time employees. For example, they help staff pizza delivery operations when it rains (and customers are more reluctant to leave their houses), run one-time events, fill in gaps when employees quit, and stock Odwalla juices at stores that have unexpectedly run out of the product. On average, Wonolo fills jobs within four hours, by pushing them to its workforce of 30,000 on their mobile phones, much as Uber routes jobs to drivers. At the end of the day, management rates workers and vice versa. "It's Uber, but for the staffing problem," AJ Brustein, Wonolo's cofounder and COO, said.[4]

Traditional temp and staffing agencies have long filled the same types of jobs as Wonolo does, but they've taken days or weeks to do so. Wonolo eventually added a more traditional staffing agency option to its business, to accommodate clients who worried about misclassification lawsuits and would rather hire temporary employees than freelancers. Adding mobile technology to the process makes using both temp labor and independent contractors easier, more efficient, and ultimately applicable in more situations.

Is this a bad thing? Maybe not. Gig economy boosters often point out that between 70% and 85% of independent contractors say they prefer to work for themselves.[5] But the type of job that has traditionally been completed by independent contractors is narrowly defined and, most important, *highly skilled*. In the future, this may change. Deliveroo workers—whom the UK Central Arbitration Committee ruled in 2017 were legitimately self-employed—are, for instance, not well-paid professionals who can likely afford to create their own safety nets, but couriers. As the potential for companies to use independent contractors expands with mobile technology and automation, it's possible that workers could regard new types of piecemeal labor as being more like temp work. Unlike free-lancers, 77% of temp workers say they would rather have a traditional full-time job.[6]

At TechCrunch Disrupt, Dan and Oisin clutched bottles of conference-branded water and crossed their legs, each resting a foot on a knee. Rather than answer the question about whether the gig economy was over, Oisin argued over semantics. These new developments shouldn't be called the gig economy, he said, punctuating every beat with his free hand. What they really do is remove friction from business transactions. He hadn't exactly suggested a new name for the gig economy, but the moderator joked about the "frictionless economy."

"Dan, what do you think of the new name?"

Dan shrugged with his hands. "Oisin makes a good point," he said.

The conversation did not become any more direct from there. Oisin, who in public appearances could sound rehearsed, as if he were reciting a political speech, repeated the "gig econ-omy is flexibility" mantra. Dan, a bit more natural on stage but still sticking to his talking points, recited his Good Jobs

Strategy spiel. Oisin attributed the lawsuits Handy has faced to "lawyers who want to make a quick buck." Dan noted that there's no reason that flexibility has to mean that workers give up the protections of being an employee—there's no law stopping companies from letting employees pick their own schedules.

It was the same conversation they had been having separately for years. But the businesses they'd built around it had completely transformed.

Managed by Q had raised another $55 million in funding and begun rolling out a new portion of its business that functioned more like the gig economy. Office managers could use the feature "marketplace" to order services like office staffing, catering, maintenance, IT help, and cleaning. Though Managed by Q still had its own office operators in New York, Los Angeles, and Chicago, this new product worked a lot like the first version of Q, with small businesses, rather than Managed by Q employees, handling the work. So far, about 200 businesses had signed up to sell through the platform.

Q's marketplace wasn't quite an Uber-like experience. In some ways, it was more like Yelp: Clients browsed profiles of the small businesses to make decisions about who to hire, and they could hire the same company repeatedly if they liked the service, while workers were typically employees of the small businesses rather than independent contractors. But Managed by Q did take a 10% to 20% cut of the bill when office managers ordered services using the marketplace, similar to the way that Handy and Uber take a cut from their independent contractors. In newly launched cities, Managed by Q had not yet decided whether it would hire its own operators or whether it would merely use its technology platform to connect offices with small businesses.

Managed by Q had proven that a cleaning and handyman company could be profitable while treating its workers well. What made it attractive as a technology company was that it could expand by routing work to other businesses.

Handy, meanwhile, had installed a new training process for cleaners that could be completed entirely online and added more automated layers to its customer service lines, both of which had cut down on the cost of acquiring cleaners and customers. It had, according to the *Inc.* article, stopped speed-scaling and focused instead on building a critical mass in the cities where it already operated.

Throughout this process, the company's executives continued to advocate for new laws that addressed its on-demand workforce. Though their efforts toward an on-demand-worker bill in New York State had not resulted in policy changes, its executives remained vocal about what they saw as archaic laws that prevented them from offering workers more support. The problem, Oisin had argued in a *Wired* op-ed headlined "We Must Protect the Gig Economy to Protect the Future of Work," was that "the current regulations never contemplated these new ways to work."[7]

Why hadn't Handy, Jon wanted to know, been more vocal about the dismantling of the Affordable Care Act? After Donald Trump was elected president, congressional Republicans made it clear they planned to repeal the US law, which made it easier for the independent contractors that Handy relied on to buy their own insurance. Oisin didn't answer the question. "There's a massive amount of uncertainty," he said.

But doesn't this effect your workforce? Jon asked Oisin about the Affordable Care Act.

"It's a very serious issue," Oisin said, dodging the question for a second time.

Jon's next very direct question essentially amounted to: Isn't the gig economy a way to take money from frontline workers and turn it into profits for tech entrepreneurs?

"I think we are in danger of that, but we are all actively working to solve that problem," Oisin said. He seemed to be referencing the drafted New York State bill Handy had circulated a year earlier, which proposed a safe harbor for gig economy companies that contributed to workers' benefit funds. Months later, Handy would lobby—successfully in some states—for legislation that similarly protected it from misclassification lawsuits, but did not include any requirement to create benefits for workers.

Handy wasn't the only gig economy company that talked about efforts to improve the experience of workers on their platforms. Care.com, a website for hiring nannies, babysitters, and other caregivers, with 26.4 million registered users worldwide, had, for instance, experimented with a benefits platform that took a percentage of transactions paid to workers and put it into a fund that workers could use to pay for healthcare, sick days, and other benefits. Uber had also experimented with the idea of a portable benefit. It structured one pilot program somewhat similarly to the Black Car Fund in New York, which provides more than 70,000 livery drivers—typically, like Uber drivers, independent contractors—with workers' compensation insurance via a 2.5% surcharge on every ride. The customer pays into the fund, rather than the dispatcher. Uber's version raised rates on some rides by about 5 cents per mile and gave drivers an option to put that additional 5 cents per mile into a benefits fund that in the event of an accident would cover medical expenses, lost income, or survivors' benefits.

Additional startups had meanwhile rushed to fill in some of the security that work increasingly lacked. An app called Even helped employees with unpredictable schedules plan for the uneven income. Whenever a worker was paid less than her average, Even deposited extra money in her account, interest-free. When she made more than her average, Even paid itself back. It created the semblance of steady income. Even eventually partnered with Walmart to give employees an option to receive part of their paycheck before their two-week pay period was over, helping them avoid payday loans if they faced an unexpected expense. Another startup called Honest Dollar provided retirement savings accounts for independent workers. It offered a $5 monthly discount to drivers for Lyft, which introduced it in a blog post as "an easy, affordable investing platform built with independent contractors in mind."[8] (Goldman Sachs acquired Honest Dollar four months later.)

An organization called Peers.org aimed to collect these sorts of services onto a single platform and to entice companies to participate by contributing to benefits like healthcare and retirement savings. "You know when you start a new job, and they hand you a folder filled with all of your benefits, and it's not scary?" its director at the time, Shelby Clark, asked me. "Like that, but in an app." Clark later said he hadn't found many companies willing to divert pay into worker funds. Most startups had been afraid that participating would make them susceptible to misclassification lawsuits. (Peers eventually merged with another organization that advocates for on-demand workers.)

The problems with many efforts that aimed to close gaps in security for workers were, first, that their results paled in comparison to the security of a traditional full-time job with benefits, and, second, that they involved a choice. Companies that hired independent contractors could choose whether to participate in a benefits fund like the one Peers.org had envisioned. They could choose to ensure contract workers were paid at least $15 per hour, as Facebook does. And they could choose whether to listen to workers' complaints or to listen to workers at all. All of these were choices that, given customer demands for dirt-cheap service no matter what the cost to workers and the threat of misclassification lawsuits, companies weren't likely to make.

Contract work, freelancing, and outsourcing can all involve good treatment and compensation. But relying on good actors to make decisions that benefit workers is not a scalable solution. While the Good Jobs Strategy may have been successfully embraced by companies like Managed by Q, one need only take a look at how many employees have access to sick days (65%) and paid family leave (13%)—neither of which is mandated by US law—to see that the strategy doesn't cover everyone.[9] There may be a way to make good jobs a profitable choice, but there will also always be some employers who don't choose it. In the gig economy, those employers have very few mandated obligations to workers.

Fixing this problem involves more than cracking down on companies that cheat workers by incorrectly calling them non-employees. The gig economy has, in addition to creating gray areas of control, expanded the ranks of the legitimately independent. Gig work platforms that target a particular industry, like Gigster, where Curtis signed up to work, deliver specific expertise on demand. And those like Mechanical Turk make it possible to chop jobs into individual gigs and disperse them to a crowd. It's easier than ever to get work done without hiring someone as an employee. But the growing group of non-traditional workers that results has no access to labor protections or safety nets provided by law to employees. And all of the misclassification lawsuits in the world aren't going to change that.

At TechCrunch Disrupt, the conversation between Dan and Oisin ultimately turned to this bigger structural problem. As Jon started moving on to the next question, Dan interrupted to give his own answer to the question of whether the gig economy was just shifting profits from frontline workers to employers. Though the (now former) secretary of labor had a year earlier told Managed by Q's employees that their efforts were building the middle class in America, Dan pointed elsewhere. "I think we have to be eyes wide open to the reality that we live in a world where wealth perpetuates wealth and poverty perpetuates poverty," he said. "There's a big conversation to have about how to build the middle class in America, and I don't think that it's honestly something that Oisin and I can solve."

EPILOGUE

WEALTH PERPETUATES WEALTH, BUT IN-DEMAND SKILLS
do, too. Curtis Larson, the New York City programmer, didn't
pay much attention to debates over the gig economy, though
he shared the independent contractor status of Uber drivers
and Handy cleaners. He had no reason to pay attention, because
the gig economy worked great for him.

His success was just as true as the Dumas program's failure. Curtis had worked hard to set up his small freelancing
business on the site Gigster, and it regularly routed programming jobs to him. He was able to maintain his previous wage
and live the flexible "vacation on a moment's notice" lifestyle
that had lured him in the first place. And yet, the last time I
talked with him, in July of 2016, he was about to sign an employment contract with Silicon Valley's golden child, SpaceX,
a Los Angeles–based startup created by Elon Musk that builds
rockets and spacecraft. It was a surprise to both of us.

"It's the only company I would want to work for instead
of freelancing," Curtis said. "It's pretty much a dream company." On a live video feed in 2013, he'd watched SpaceX test
its first reusable rocket, *Grasshopper,* and he'd kept tabs on its

progress ever since. The work SpaceX did seemed more mean-ingful than most of the startups he'd been exposed to, which worked on new ways to serve online ads or advertised them-selves as Uber for delivering pet supplies. "We don't know very much about anything outside of Earth; space has the biggest mysteries of life," Curtis said, before admitting a beat later, "and I just think it's really cool."

Working at SpaceX had been Curtis's dream: something he thought about in an abstract way but never imagined would be a realistic option. Then, one day in May, he had finished his freelancing work at the coffee shop and realized something had changed. He'd spent the last year teaching himself, through freelance work, how to tackle a broader range of projects. And suddenly he felt qualified. He filled out the online application.

He was shocked when SpaceX called him back. Three tech-nical phone interviews later, he was flying to Los Angeles to meet the team in person. The software engineers worked on the same campus as the engineers who were building the rock-ets, and on the factory tour he saw the shop space where they built rocket bodies and the clean rooms where they worked on electronics and space suits.

Curtis wouldn't earn as much money at SpaceX as he had as a freelancer, and he'd been warned that SpaceX employees worked a hard schedule—about 11 hours per day, at a mini-mum. The snacks didn't even stack up to those at his last full-time job. But he'd be working on *space travel*.

The time Curtis spent freelancing had provided him with not only the new skills he needed to land his dream job, but a new sense of security. "If I really don't like working for them," he figured, "it will be really easy to quit and go back to free-lancing." He might even pick up an occasional project on the weekend, if he got bored or just needed some beer money.

This is why then–Uber CEO Travis Kalanick had called the gig economy a "safety net." For Curtis, it really was.

Forming a cooperative version of Mechanical Turk started to look less feasible for Kristy as she continued her education. She didn't love academia, and she no longer wanted to get a Ph.D., which had been the context in which she had planned to build the platform. At a conference, she'd run into the founder of a digital cooperative called Fairmondo, and he'd told her that he thought he'd be running it forever.

That made her pause. Kristy didn't want to run a platform forever. She also didn't want to be poor forever. Her husband wouldn't be able to work into old age doing physical labor, and she had much less time to make money before retirement than her 20-something classmates.

After finishing her master's degree in labor studies, she decided to become a lawyer. I visited her in Toronto the week after she took the LSAT. We sat in her apartment living room, under a huge poster of Paris, while her dogs yapped in the other room. "Stop!" she'd shout at them every once in a while, which seemed to calm them down, as though they had only been inquiring whether she was still there.

Just before the LSAT, her arm injuries started acting up

again. She worried about holding a pencil for the test. Her husband had in the meantime named her elbow brace a "Mechanical Turk badge of honor." She'd avoided painkillers out of fear they would impact her ability to study effectively.

Though she was still nervous about how she'd done on the test when I visited, she ended up scoring well enough on the exam to earn admittance to two Toronto law schools. As a lawyer, she was hoping she'd be able to advocate for workers and make money at the same time—that she wouldn't have to give up what, perhaps, was one of her greatest talents: "I say things that people don't want to hear," she explained. "I say them loudly. And I say it to their face so they don't miss it."

By the summer of 2017, Abe had put all things Uber aside. After the strikes and his last-ditch attempt to sell his silence to Uber had failed, he decided to start his own ride-hailing app called A-Ryde. He spent money promoting the idea at a conference and filming a commercial ("Woaaahh, let's not ruin this night with surge pricing," a hip young man tells a friend who presumably is about to use a different ride-hailing app). When Abe couldn't raise enough funding to launch the app, he tried to sell his house to finance it (given that a lien had been placed on it, that didn't work).

Since then, he'd realized that the thought of competing with Uber, a startup with billions of dollars in funding, had always been a fantasy. Abe told me he'd grown a lot as a person since the days of Uber Freedom. He'd stopped falling for get-rich-quick schemes and started saving as much money as he could to buy more real estate. It would be real estate that would eventually make him a millionaire, he believed now. And yes, he'd found real estate gurus online, but none of them had asked him for money the way that Kevin Trudeau had or requested a percentage of each of his transactions, the way Uber had.

A $25,000 lawsuit settlement payment from a former employer allowed him to buy his second house and start collecting rent. His plan was to buy one house a year, until he could become "financially free." In case that didn't work, he'd started investing in Bitcoin.

Donald Trump's election, Abe believed, boded well for him. Abe had heard that the new president would pass laws beneficial to real estate tycoons. And he liked Trump's intentions to cut taxes on corporations. The way he saw it, both of these things would benefit him and his mission to become a millionaire.

Considering Abe's attitude toward credit card bills, which he told me he never paid, it seemed likely that his credit was completely shot. No bank would ever give him a loan. No credit card company would ever extend him a line of credit. He was probably being hounded by debt collectors, he said, but he'd installed a call-blocking app on his phone, so he wouldn't know.

Abe tried to work every day so he could save the cash to buy houses. All in all, he couldn't say he regretted believing that GIN would make him a millionaire or believing that Uber would make him a business owner. It had taught him that the only path to financial freedom would be hard and slow, and that he shouldn't believe people when they told him otherwise. The idea that he would always need to work crappy service jobs in order to make a living, that he would never become a millionaire, still wasn't one that he was even willing to entertain. "I know that for sure, without a doubt, before I turn 40 I will do it," he said.

In the meantime, he planned to keep saving. He'd try not to spend any money. Every small purchase he made was another hour he would need to spend at work before becoming financially free.

Though he had finally, at the age of 31, after five years of sleeping on an air mattress on the floor, decided to invest in a real bed.

"Oh boy oh boy oh boy oh boy," Gary Foster said when I talked with him on the phone in late 2016. I had just asked him how everything turned out. "Things turned out terrible is what they did," he told me.

Gary and I had last spoken when he'd been working as a customer service representative, the job that Terrence had helped him land. Now he was working as a truck driver. He was on his way to Washington State, sitting in the passenger seat of a truck next to his driving partner. After that he'd go to Seattle. He wouldn't be home for a month, but he was getting paid between $800 and $1,200 per week. That was more than he made at the call center, which he'd left after disputes about his pay and insufficient hours.

Other than missing his wife and son, he said, "It's ok. It's a job."

As a truck driver, Gary worked for a trucking company that contracted with other businesses. He wasn't really even aware of which company's cargo was inside of his truck. Often the contents were covered by a shield, so he couldn't see them.

To get the truck-driving job, he'd completed a monthlong course required to obtain his commercial truck-driving license. After that, there'd been a month of training. When we had first met in Dumas, he told me that he disliked his job at the Tyson factory because of the hour-long commute. "Now I'm doing nothing but driving," he said, laughing at the contradiction.

It wasn't a bad employment outcome. Gary hoped he would save enough to buy his own truck at some point, and he was thinking about moving to Milwaukee. He had always been bored in Dumas, and his mother, for whom he'd wanted to stay, had remarried and needed less help from him.

According to a 2014 study by the nonprofit National Employment Law Project, about 65% of all US port truckers are treated as employees but classified as contractors.[1] Gary was not one of them. The long-haul truck company had hired him as an employee. On its website, it advertised medical, dental, and vision insurance, a 401(k) retirement plan, accident and disability insurance, paid vacations, and free life insurance. "We've never had a layoff," the application site bragged.

It was a decent job, but not one that was likely to survive automation.

In some industries, the gig economy serves as a stop-gap technology, with companies employing people in the cheapest way possible until, eventually, it becomes cheaper to buy a machine. This is the case with Uber and Lyft, for instance. "The reason Uber could be expensive is because you're not just paying for the car—you're paying for the other dude in the car," Travis Kalanick said on stage at a conference in 2014. "When there's no other dude in the car, the cost of taking an Uber anywhere becomes cheaper than owning a vehicle."[2] Uber started picking up passengers in its first tests of self-driving cars in Pittsburgh in 2016. Toyota, Nissan, General Motors, and Google have all estimated that automated cars will be on the road by 2020.[3]

In the United States, 1.8 million people make a living driving trucks; another 687,000 drive buses; another 1.4 million deliver packages; and another 305,000 work as taxi drivers and chauffeurs. What will they do when vehicles drive themselves?

It's not just drivers who may soon see their jobs, or portions of their jobs, become automated. A recent McKinsey report estimated that almost all jobs could be automated in some respect, though the extent and impact of this automation is likely to vary widely.[4]

At some point, increasing automation will help power the gig economy, making it even more efficient than it is now. Though Curtis never talked about it, and I'm not sure he even realized it, Gigster's ultimate goal is to automate as much of the programming process as possible. "In five years, maybe we'll automate 20 percent," said Roger Dickey, the cofounder and CEO of Gigster. "In five more years, 40 percent. Five more years, 60 percent. It will never get to exactly 100 percent, until general [artificial intelligence] is created. And then the world probably ends, so we're moot on that point."

Managing roles at Gigster will be the first to go. Curtis had already received automated emails when there was a project that was appropriate for him, something that a manager might otherwise have sent. Gigster was also building an automated idea generator that would supplement its sales team's efforts, for instance, automatically reminding a client "we notice your e-commerce website has a 30% lower conversion rate than its competitors, and we found this new feature raises the conversion rate by this percentage. Click here to proceed." When they click, perhaps the feature they have selected, which is similar to others that human coders have already produced for Gigster projects, automatically appears and adjusts itself to fit into the new site. A programmer doesn't need to build it again. "There's much further we can go down that road," Dickey said. First it might take the form of a "starter template" for programmers.

That doesn't necessarily mean that Gigster won't need programmers—it just won't need programmers to do the same things they do now. Automation could mean gigs will be more interesting and easier to find. "If you walk outside, you can see that it's not like there's nothing to do," said Devin Fidler, the research director at the nonprofit Institute for the Future. "We just don't have the right assigning technology."

He envisions a "shift from people looking for jobs to jobs looking for people," with technology that will automatically match odd jobs with qualified workers—the gig economy, but spread across even more professions and jobs. "You turn it on like a tap," he said. "Rather than a huge inefficient hunt any time you want to work, work is routed to you."

If you're a software developer, this is easy to envision. But if you're a truck driver, it's not clear what those tasks would look like.

In July 2017, Dan created a personal syllabus of sorts that covered how work was changing. The results sat in two bulging canvas bags on his kitchen table. One was filled with manila folders labeled "platform economics" and "future of work." They were stuffed with white copy paper, clipped together in sections with black clamps. The other was filled with books: David Weil's book about how technology will impact jobs. A book about the second machine age. I'd chipped in a copy of *Janesville*, a book that followed a small town near where I'd grown up after the local GM assembly plant shut down, taking thousands of good jobs with it. Dan's plan was to read the entire foot-and-a-half stack during a four-day solo trip to a cabin, a goal which somehow didn't strike him at all as unrealistically ambitious.

For now, the stacks looked like something of a centerpiece in his otherwise neglected apartment, which contained a few pieces of art and framed mementos, a dusty desk with a pile of old laptop computers, a leather couch, a bed, a minimal dresser, and a single metal rack filled with shirts and blazers. There were still holes in the floor from the time he'd converted the former two-bedroom apartment into a one-bedroom apartment with a hammer, and an electrical outlet hung from the open ceiling above the former room. His couch faced a square of faded Yogi Bear wallpaper left over from the last resident.

Recently, Dan had propped up a surfboard in one corner. He'd been trying to take care of himself, go to yoga classes and take at least one day per week off from work. It wasn't necessarily easy. Sometimes during evenings and weekends he'd open Slack, the workplace chat app, hoping someone would be working so he could work, too. But he'd started meeting with an executive coach, and he'd taught himself, he felt, to be less reactive. Everyone who reported to him now got a copy of his "user manual," which attempted to explain his intense work ethic, his frustration with those who didn't try as hard as he did, and his intolerance for sugar-coated news.

The stakes of running Managed by Q had risen. At the beginning, Dan could have failed, but that wouldn't really have mattered to anyone but him and Saman. Now he had 1,000 employees to let down if anything went wrong; 220 of them, hourly employees, had just received their first stock grants.

It wasn't clear exactly what Dan had to gain by studying the "future of work" so ambitiously. Maybe he was, with his stack of books, preparing to promote Managed by Q as a good partner for small businesses, or for some future political campaign. "I like Bloomberg's style," he had told me once, referring to the billionaire and former mayor of New York City. "He cannot be bought. People can disagree with him, but they can't question his integrity."

But even if there were some self-interest in Dan's motives, I think it would still be reasonable for him to care about where our work future is headed. The full-time job—to which we've attached all of the rules about treating workers fairly—is dissolving, and the community of workers who are treated as second-class citizens, who aren't protected by the same laws or entitled to the same benefits as other workers, is growing. That is a big, scary problem, and one worth studying.

Before I left our interview, I wished Dan good luck in the woods. Then, just as more than 40 million people around the world do every month, I took out my smartphone and ordered an Uber.[5] A driver named Abid drove me home. He usually drove all night, he told me, because that's when his app tended to pay the most.

From the time I first heard about the gig economy until I finished writing this book, I spent nearly six years observing a sector of the economy that brought together the tremendous hopes of Silicon Valley and the disappointing reality that our support systems are not prepared to handle the major changes on the horizon.

At the end of it, I don't think Silicon Valley was wrong to attempt to restructure the job. Our current model wasn't working, and the startup spirit of experimentation was necessary. But attempting to tackle the problems of the job—and yes, delivering flexibility—without fixing the support structures around it can't quite count as progress, and it certainly doesn't look like innovation.

The last time our country had to reconstruct a safety net from scratch, technological progress had, much like today, just upended the way work was structured. As American workers flocked from independent rural farms and businesses to city-centered factories during the Industrial Revolution, work developed assigned hours, a central location, and a hierarchical structure. As with the evolution of work today, this change wasn't immediately wonderful.

Early factory workers spent 12- and 14-hour days toiling away in putrid conditions, which sometimes included breathing in smoke from whale-oil lamps (the windows were often nailed shut). As a society, we sent kids to work, locked workers inside of buildings so that they couldn't take unapproved breaks (or, you know, escape if there was a fire), and allowed employers to pay starvation wages.

We made the same arguments for change then as we could make today. Samuel Gompers, the first president of the AFL, wrote in 1894 that when the Constitution had been written more than 100 years prior:

> Men knew scarcely anything of the existence of the power of steam; they knew nothing at all of electricity; they had no suspicion even in the days of Adam Smith of the steam engine and the electric motor or the telegraph, the telephone, the application of steam and electricity to industry; and yet the laws that had been made in the period ... are sought to be applied to modern industry and modern commerce ... I submit that industry and commerce cannot go back to conform to old thoughts, old theories, and old crusty customs of law, but that the law, sooner, must be changed to conform to the changed industrial and commercial conditions.[6]

The solution was not to force workers out of factories and back onto farms. It took another half century or so for the labor movement, in partnership with government and private industry, to form things like a standard ten-hour day (despite mill owners' argument that greater leisure time would leave workers susceptible to corrupting influences), state laws regulating child labor, and requirements for worker safety. It took until the 1930s for New Deal legislation to create programs like Social Security, unemployment insurance, the minimum wage, and disability insurance.

The gig economy, it turns out, is not the on-demand improvement to the "future of work" that its creators once imagined. But it will play an important role in exemplifying what that future might look like, and the slow, hard work that we must do to prepare for it.

Acknowledgments

I am grateful to the people who shared their time and stories with me for this book. Without them, it wouldn't have been possible.

Terrence Davenport, a great teacher in his classroom, was also a patient and kind teacher to me. Kristy Milland stuck with me during several busy times in her life, somehow still managing to return my emails within 15 minutes. Curtis Larson, whom I met at a coworking meetup, was generous enough to answer my phone calls even years later. And Dan Teran continued to make time for interviews even as his company grew in size, from our first interview to our last, by at least a factor of ten.

Thank you also to Gary Foster, Rina Patel, Anthony Knox, Abe Husein, and Saman Rahmanian for sharing their perspectives with me during interviews, and to Ethan Pollack, Six Silberman, and Palak Shah for helping me parse unfamiliar topics. Thank you to Amy Goldstein for giving advice to a stranger.

David Lidsky started the chain of events that ultimately resulted in this book, one of the more significant favors anyone has done me. I am also grateful to *Fast Company* and *Quartz*, my employers, for their support; to my editor, Tim Bartlett, both for seeing potential in this story and for helping to shape it; and to my agent, Alia Hanna Habib, who has also been a much-appreciated source of feedback.

At St. Martin's, I'd like to thank Alan Bradshaw for improving this book throughout its final stages, Jennifer Simington for her thoughtful copy edit, and Alice Pfeifer for her help throughout the long editing process.

Writing this book would have been much more difficult without the support of several extraordinary people in my life. My parents were, in a sense, my first editors, and they have been a source of ceaseless encouragement for as long as I can remember. I am so lucky. Thank you also to my brother, grandparents, aunts, uncles, and cousins, who were all supportive enough to be excited about this project, but kind enough to not remind me of my deadline over the holidays; to the Schwartz family; to Emily; and to Marguerite.

A special thank you to Alex, who served as proofreader, chef, and therapist as needed. Your confidence in me has made all the difference.

Notes

PREFACE

1 Katz, Lawrence F., and Alan B. Krueger. The Rise and Nature of Alternative Work Arrangements in the United States, 1995–2015. National Bureau of Economic Research Working Paper 22667. 2016.

2 Kessler, Sarah. Online Odd Jobs: How Startups Let You Fund Yourself. *Mashable*. December 29, 2011. http://mashable.com/2011/12/29/new-working-economy/.

CHAPTER 1

1 Kessler, Sarah. 13 Potential Breakout Apps to Watch at South by Southwest 2011. *Mashable*. March 9, 2011. http://mashable.com/2011/03/09/startups-to-watch-sxsw/#bexrtH8S0kqo.

2 Kessler, Sarah. Who's Nearby? This App Lets You Know. *Mashable*. January 24, 2012. http://mashable.com/2012/01/24/highlight/#iasBqOnotuqA.

3 Tiku, Nitasha. Leaked: Uber's Internal Revenue and Ride Request Numbers. *ValleyWag*. December 4, 2013. http://valleywag.gawker.com/leaked-ubers-internal-revenue-and-ride-request-number-14759 24182.

4 Actual salaries and wages comprise only 69.4% of an employer's hourly cost for hiring a worker in the United States. Employers on

average pay an additional 7.8% in federally required and state-required benefits like Social Security and Medicare and another 13.5% in other benefits such as healthcare (these percentages vary between industries).

Hallock, Kevin. *Pay: Why People Earn What They Earn and What You Can Do Now to Make More*. Cambridge University Press, 2012.

5 Uber Newsroom. New Survey: Drivers Choose Uber for Its Flexibility and Convenience. December 7, 2015. https://newsroom.uber .com/driver-partner-survey/.

6 Quoted in Hatton, Erin. The Rise of the Permanent Temp Economy. *New York Times*. January 26, 2013. https://opinionator.blogs .nytimes.com/2013/01/26/the-rise-of-the-permanent-temp -economy/.

7 Dey, Matthew, Susan Houseman, and Anne Polivka. What Do We Know about Contracting Out in the United States? Evidence from Household and Establishment Surveys. In *Labor in the New Economy*, eds. Katharine G. Abraham, James R. Spletzer, and Michael Harper. University of Chicago Press, October 2010.

8 Manyika, James, Susan Lund, Jacques Bughin, Kelsey Robinson, Jan Mischke, and Deepa Mahajan. *Independent Work: Choice, Necessity, and the Gig Economy*. McKinsey Global Institute. October 2016.

9 General Accounting Office. *Contingent Workforce: Size, Characteristics, Earnings, and Benefits*, GAO-15-168R. April 2015. Available from: http://www.gao.gov/products/GAO-15-168R.

10 Tiku, Leaked: Uber's Internal Revenue.

11 Ibid.

12 Tsotsis, Alexia. TaskRabbit Gets $13M from Founders Fund and Others to "Revolutionize the World's Labor Force." *TechCrunch*. July 23, 2012.

CHAPTER 2

[1] Melendez, Steven. How Uber Conquered the World in 2013. *Fast Company*. January 3, 2014. https://www.fastcompany.com/3024236/how-uber-conquered-the-world-in-2013.

[2] Uber has offered as much as $2,500 for a referral that meets specific conditions, such as the new driver has a taxi license and also signs up with Uber's partner to rent a car for 12 months.

[3] Trudeau, Kevin. *Your Wish Is Your Command*. Audiobook. Global Information Network, 2009.

[4] Meisner, Jason. TV Pitchman Kevin Trudeau Sentenced to 10 Years in Prison. *Chicago Tribune*. March 17, 2014. http://www.chicagotribune.com/business/chi-kevin-trudeau-sentenced-20140317-story.html.

[5] Uber eventually shut Xchange down after it discovered it was losing 18 times more money per vehicle than it originally had thought.

[6] Griswold, Alison. Inside Uber's Unsettling Alliance with Some of New York's Shadiest Car Dealers. *Quartz*. June 27, 2017. https://qz.com/1013882/ubers-rental-and-lease-programs-with-new-york-car-dealers-push-drivers-toward-shady-subprime-contracts/.

[7] Taylor, Kate. Why Millenials Are Ending the 9 to 5. *Forbes*. August 23, 2013. https://www.forbes.com/sites/katetaylor/2013/08/23/why-millennials-are-ending-the-9-to-5/#55af647c715d.

[8] Agan, Tom. Embracing the Millennials' Mind-Set at Work. *New York Times*. November 9, 2013. http://www.nytimes.com/2013/11/10/jobs/embracing-the-millennials-mind-set-at-work.html.

[9] Matchar, Emily. How Those Spoiled Millennials Will Make the Workplace Better for Everyone. *Washington Post*. August 16, 2012. https://www.washingtonpost.com/opinions/how-those-spoiled-millennials-will-make-the-workplace-better-for-everyone/2012/08/16/814af692-d5d8-11e1-a0cc-8954acd5f90c_story.html?utm_term=.26a74c545bef.

10 Fry, Richard. Millennials Surpass Gen Xers as the Largest Generation in the U.S. Labor Force. Pew Research Center. May 11, 2015. http://www.pewresearch.org/fact-tank/2015/05/11/millennials -surpass-gen-xers-as-the-largest-generation-in-u-s-labor-force/.

11 It's called Coase's Theory of the Firm.

12 Manyika, James, Susan Lund, Jacques Bughin, Kelsey Robinson, Jan Mischke, and Deepa Mahajan. *Independent Work: Choice, Necessity, and the Gig Economy*. McKinsey Global Institute. October 2016.

13 From https://gigster.com; since changed.

14 Kalil, Tom, and Farnamn Jahanian. Computer Science Is for Everyone! Obama White House Archives. December 11, 2013. https://obamawhitehouse.archives.gov/blog/2013/12/11/computer -science-everyone.

15 Kessler, Sarah. Tech Interns at Facebook and Snapchat Make Significantly More Than Almost All Americans. *Quartz*. December 5, 2016. https://qz.com/851945/how-much-interns-at-tech-companies -get-paid/.

16 Though Gigster in 2016 announced it would offer freelance workers a way to earn equity in some of the startups they collectively did work for, Curtis never heard anything about how to participate.

CHAPTER 3

1 "20% of full-time freelancers": Murphy, Laura. What to Do about Health Care? The Conversation on Both Sides of the Aisle. *Freelancers Union* (blog). November 3, 2016. https://blog.freelancersunion .org/2016/11/03/health-insurance-2016. "10.3% of the non-elderly general population": The Henry J. Kaiser Family Foundation. Key Facts about the Uninsured Population. September 19, 2017. http://kff .org/uninsured/fact-sheet/key-facts-about-the-uninsured-population

l. The Affordable Care drastically reduced the number of people who go without health insurance. During the ten years before the policy was implemented in 2014, the rate hovered at about 16%.

2 Manyika, James, Susan Lund, Jacques Bughin, Kelsey Robinson, Jan Mischke, and Deepa Mahajan. *Independent Work: Choice, Necessity, and the Gig Economy.* McKinsey Global Institute. October 2016.

3 Arrington, Michael. Amazon Finally Reveals Itself as the Matrix. *TechCrunch.* November 4, 2005. https://techcrunch.com/2005/11/04/amazon-finally-shows-itself-as-the-matrix/.

4 Berg, Janine. Income Security in the On-Demand Economy: Findings and Policy Lessons from a Survey of Crowdworkers. International Labour Office. 2016.

CHAPTER 4

1 Weiner, Jenna. What Does oDesk Mean Anyway? Our Startup Story. *Upwork Blog.* March 26, 2013. https://www.upwork.com/blog/2013/03/what-does-odesk-mean-anyway-our-startup-story/.

2 Dey, Matthew, Susan Houseman, and Anne Polivka. What Do We Know about Contracting Out in the United States? Evidence from Household and Establishment Surveys. In *Labor in the New Economy,* eds. Katharine G. Abraham, James R. Spletzer, and Michael Harper. University of Chicago Press, October 2010.

CHAPTER 5

1 Farrell, Diana, and Fiona Greig. Paychecks, Paydays, and the Online Platform Economy. JP Morgan Chase & Co. Institute. February 2016.

2 Squawk Box. CNBC. Wednesday, April 27, 2016. Transcript available from: http://www.cnbc.com/2016/04/27/cnbc-exclusive-cnbc

-excerpts-uber-co-founder-ceo-travis-kalanick-on-cnbcs-squawk
-box-today.html.

3 Kokalitcheva, Kia. Uber's CEO Calls His Company a Labor
"Safety Net." *Fortune*. June 24, 2016. http://fortune.com/2016/06/23
/uber-safety-net-comments/.

4 Upwork press release. Freelancers Union and Upwork Release New
Study Revealing Insights into the Almost 54 Million People Freelancing in America. October 1, 2015. https://www.upwork.com/press/2015
/10/01/freelancers-union-and-upwork-release-new-study-revealing
-insights-into-the-almost-54-million-people-freelancing-in-america/.

5 Hanrahan, Disin. We Must Protect the On-Demand Economy to
Protect the Future of Work. *Wired*. November 9, 2015. http://www
.wired.com/2015/11/we-must-protect-the-on-demand-economy
-to-protect-the-future-of-work/.

6 Wheeler, Brian. Gig Economy Workers "Like the Flexibility." BBC.
October 5, 2017. http://www.bbc.com/news/uk-politics-41490172.

7 Working Mothers Issue Brief. Women's Bureau US Department
of Labor. June 2016. https://www.dol.gov/wb/resources/WB_Working
Mothers_508_FinalJune13.pdf.

8 Hochschild, Arlie, and Anne Machung. *The Second Shift*. Penguin
Books. 2013. It is no surprise that more women, who still bear an
unequal share of caregiving responsibilities, are more likely to say
that flexibility is important to them. In one UK survey, 40% of women
said that flexible working is "very important" to them in contrast to
23% of men. Similarly, 42% of people of all genders who have caring
responsibilities said flexible working was important in comparison
to 29% of those without caring responsibilities.

9 Press release. International Labour Organization. September 6,
1999. http://www.ilo.org/global/about-the-ilo/newsroom/news
/WCMS_071326/lang—en/index.htm. Despite this increase in hours
for full-time workers, the average number of hours worked in the

United States is falling slightly, as many workers, especially those with less education and less elite jobs, struggle to find as much work as they would like.

10 US Employee Engagement, 2011–2015. Gallup Daily tracking interviews. http://news.gallup.com/poll/188144/employee-engagement-stagnant-2015.aspx.

11 US Bureau of Labor Statistics. https://data.bls.gov/timeseries/LNS14000000.

12 Desilver, Drew. US Income Inequality, on Rise for Decades, Is Now Highest since 1928. Pew Research Center. December 5, 2013. http://www.pewresearch.org/fact-tank/2013/12/05/u-s-income-inequality-on-rise-for-decades-is-now-highest-since-1928/.

13 Friedman, Thomas. How to Monetize Your Closet. *New York Times*. December 21, 2013. http://www.nytimes.com/2013/12/22/opinion/sunday/friedman-how-to-monetize-your-closet.html; Geron, Tomio. Airbnb and the Unstoppable Rise of the Share Economy. *Forbes*. February 11, 2013. http://www.forbes.com/sites/tomiogeron/2013/01/23/airbnb-and-the-unstoppable-rise-of-the-share-economy/#463a65b6790b.

14 Johnson, Justin Elof. Will You Leave Your Job to Join the Sharing Economy? *VentureBeat*. January 21, 2013. http://venturebeat.com/2013/01/21/will-you-leave-your-job-to-join-the-sharing-economy/.

15 Manjoo, Farhad. Uber's Business Model Could Change Your Work. *New York Times*. January 28, 2015. https://www.nytimes.com/2015/01/29/technology/personaltech/uber-a-rising-business-model.html.

16 Retelny, Daniela, Sébastien Robaszkiewicz, Alexandra To, Walter S. Lasecki, Jay Patel, Negar Rahmati, Tulsee Doshi, Melissa Valentine, and Michael S. Bernstein. Expert Crowdsourcing with Flash Teams. Proceedings of the 27th Annual ACM Symposium on User Interface Software and Technology. Honolulu, Hawaii, USA. October 5–8, 2014.

17 Fidler, Devin. Here's How Managers Can Be Replaced by Software. *Harvard Business Review*. April 21, 2015. https://hbr.org/2015/04/heres-how-managers-can-be-replaced-by-software.

18 De La Merced, Michael J. Uber Attains Eye-Popping New Levels of Funding. *New York Times*. June 6, 2014. https://dealbook.nytimes.com/2014/06/06/uber-raises-new-funds-at-17-billion-valuation/.

19 Saitto, Serena. Uber Valued at $40 Billion in $1.2 Billion Equity Funding. *Bloomberg*. December 4, 2014. https://www.bloomberg.com/news/articles/2014-12-04/uber-valued-at-40-billion-with-1-2-billion-equity-fundraising.

20 Shieber, Jonathan. Handy Hits $1 Million a Week in Bookings as Cleaning Economy Consolidates. *TechCrunch*. October 14, 2014. https://techcrunch.com/2014/10/14/handy-hits-1-million-a-week-in-bookings-as-cleaning-economy-consolidates/.

CHAPTER 6

1 Bureau of Labor Statistics. Employee Benefits Survey. March 2017. https://www.bls.gov/ncs/ebs/benefits/2017/ownership/civilian/table32a.htm.

2 Berg, Janine. Income Security in the On-Demand Economy: Findings and Policy Lessons from a Survey of Crowdworkers. International Labour Office. 2016.

3 The IBO Gary worked for declined to comment on this.

CHAPTER 7

1 DePillis, Lydia. At the Uber for Home Cleaning, Workers Pay a Price for Convenience. *Washington Post*. September 10, 2014. https://

www.washingtonpost.com/news/storyline/wp/2014/09/10/at-the
-uber-for-home-cleaning-workers-pay-a-price-for-convenience/
?utm_term=.9e26416360e0.

2 Khaleeli, Homa. The Truth about Working for Deliveroo, Uber,
and the On-Demand Economy. *The Guardian*. June 2016. https://
www.theguardian.com/money/2016/jun/15/he-truth-about-working
-for-deliveroo-uber-and-the-on-demand-economy.

3 Smith, Aaron. Gig Work, Online Selling and Home Sharing. Pew
Research Center. 2016. See "Appendix: Profile of Gig Earners and
Online Sellers." http://www.pewinternet.org/2016/11/17/gig-work
-online-selling-and-home-sharing.

4 The New York Times Editorial Board. The Gig Economy's False
Promises. *New York Times*. April 10, 2017. https://www.nytimes
.com/2017/04/10/opinion/the-gig-economys-false-promise.html.

5 Greenhouse, Steven. *The Big Squeeze*. Anchor Books, 2008,
page 119.

6 Berlinski, Samuel. Wages and Contracting Out: Does the Law of
One Price Hold? *British Journal of Industrial Relations*, vol. 46. November 2007. Pages 59–75.

7 Dube, Arindrajit, and Ethan Kaplan. Institute for Research on
Labor and Employment Working Paper Series: Does Outsourcing
Reduce Wages in the Low Wage Service Occupations? Evidence
from Janitors and Guards. 2008.

8 US Government Accountability Office. *Contingent Workforce:
Size, Characteristics, Earnings, and Benefits*. April 20, 2015.

9 Weil, David. *The Fissured Workplace: Why Work Became So Bad
for So Many*. Harvard University Press, 2014, page 20.

10 Ibid., pages 76–77.

11 Wong, Julia Carrie. Facebook's Underclass: As Staffers Enjoy

Lavish Perks, Contractors Barely Get By. *The Guardian*. September 26, 2017.

12 ProPublica. How We Calculated Injury Rates for Temp and Non-Temp Workers. December 18, 2013. https://www.propublica.org/nerds /how-we-calculated-injury-rates-for-temp-and-non-temp-workers.

13 Murphy, Brett. Rigged. *USA Today*. June 16, 2017. https://www .usatoday.com/pages/interactives/news/rigged-forced-into-debt -worked-past-exhaustion-left-with-nothing/.

14 Testimony of Catherine K. Ruckelshaus, National Employment Law Project Hearing before the United States Congress Senate Committee on Health, Education, Labor & Pensions. June 17, 2010.

15 Mas, Alexandre, and Amanda Pallais. Valuing Alternative Work Arrangements. NBER Working Paper No. 22708. September 2016.

16 Kessler, Sarah. The Vast Majority of Workers Just Want a Regular Job, Not Flexibility. *Quartz*. December 15, 2016. https://qz.com /863618/workers-do-not-value-flexibility/.

CHAPTER 8

1 *Employers Do Not Always Follow Internal Revenue Service Worker Determination Rulings*. Treasury Inspector General for Tax Administration. June 14, 2013. Retrieved from http://www.treasury .gov/tigta/auditreports/2013reports/201330058fr.pdf.

2 Weil, David. "Lots of Employees Get Misclassified. Here's Why It Matters." *Harvard Business Review*. July 5, 2017. https://hbr.org /2017/07/lots-of-employees-get-misclassified-as-contractors-heres -why-it-matters.

3 Gandel, Stephen. Uber-nomics: Here's What It Would Cost Uber to Pay Its Drivers as Employees. *Fortune*. September 17, 2015. http:// fortune.com/2015/09/17/ubernomics/. And on Lyft see: Levine, Dan,

and Heather Somerville. Lyft Drivers, If Employees, Owed Millions More—Court Documents. Reuters. March 20, 2016. https://www.reuters.com/article/us-lyft-drivers-pay-exclusive/exclusive-lyft-drivers-if-employees-owed-millions-more-court-documents-idUSKCN0WM0NO?feedType=RSS&feedName=technology News.

4 Chayka, Kyle. It's Like Uber for Janitors, with One Huge Difference. *Bloomberg*. October 9, 2015. https://www.bloomberg.com/news/features/2015-10-09/it-s-like-uber-for-janitors-with-one-big-difference%0A.

5 Kessler, Sarah. Why a New Generation of Uber for X Businesses Rejected the Uber for X Model. *Fast Company*. March 29, 2016. https://www.fastcompany.com/3058299/why-a-new-generation-of-on-demand-businesses-rejected-the-uber-model.

6 Scheiber, Noam. How Uber Uses Psychological Tricks to Push Its Drivers' Buttons. *New York Times*. April 2, 2017. https://www.nytimes.com/interactive/2017/04/02/technology/uber-drivers-psychological-tricks.html.

7 Rosenblat, Alex, and Luke Stark. Algorithmic Labor and Information Asymmetries: A Case Study of Uber's Drivers. *International Journal of Communication*, vol. 10. July 2016. Page 27. http://ijoc.org/index.php/ijoc/article/view/4892/1739.

8 Alonzo, Austin. Uber Slashes Prices in KC, 47 Other Markets. *Kansas City Business Journal*. January 12, 2015. https://www.bizjournals.com/kansascity/news/2015/01/12/uber-slashes-prices.html.

9 Beating the Winter Slump: Price Cuts for Riders with Guaranteed Earnings for Drivers. January 8, 2015. https://www.uber.com/newsroom/beating-the-winter-slump-price-cuts-for-riders-and-guaranteed-earnings-for-drivers/.

10 Huet, Ellen. Uber's Clever, Hidden Move: How Its Latest Fare Cuts Can Actually Lock in Its Drivers. *Forbes*. January 9, 2015. https://

www.forbes.com/sites/ellenhuet/2015/01/09/ubers-clever-hidden
-move-how-fare-cuts-actually-lock-in-its-drivers/#66f9ad3a4f1a.

11 *Businesswire*. An Uber Impact: 20,000 Jobs Created on the Uber
Platform Every Month. May 27, 2014. https://www.businesswire
.com/news/home/20140527005594/en/Uber-Impact-20000-Jobs
-Created-Uber-Platform.

12 McFarland, Matt. Uber's Remarkable Growth Could End the Era
of Poorly Paid Cab Drivers. *Washington Post*. May 27, 2014. https://
www.washingtonpost.com/news/innovations/wp/2014/05/27
/ubers-remarkable-growth-could-end-the-era-of-poorly-paid-cab
-drivers/?utm_term=.0350a1ed0a2d.

13 Walmart press release. More Than One Million Walmart Asso-
ciates to Receive Pay Increase in 2016. January 20, 2016. https://news
.walmart.com/news-archive/2016/01/20/more-than-one-million
-walmart-associates-receive-pay-increase-in-2016.

14 O'Donovan, Caroline, and Jeremy Singer-Vine. How Much Uber
Drivers Actually Make per Hour. *BuzzFeed News*. June 22, 2016.
https://www.buzzfeed.com/carolineodonovan/internal-uber-driver
-pay-numbers?utm%5C_term=.xlBQXPj7P8&utm_term=.bjj7x
MyYJ#.sp184dxLD.

15 Isaac, Mike. Uber's C.E.O. Plays with Fire. *New York Times*.
April 23, 2017. https://www.nytimes.com/2017/04/23/technology
/travis-kalanick-pushes-uber-and-himself-to-the-precipice.html?
_r=0.

16 Federal Trade Commission website. Uber Agrees to Pay $20 Mil-
lion to Settle FTC Charges That It Recruited Prospective Drivers
with Exaggerated Earnings Claims. January 19, 2017. https://www
.ftc.gov/news-events/press-releases/2017/01/uber-agrees-pay-20
-million-settle-ftc-charges-it-recruited.

17 Green, Carla, and Sam Levin. Homeless, Assaulted, Broke:
Drivers Left behind as Uber Promises Change at the Top. *The*

Guardian. June 17, 2017. https://www.theguardian.com/us-news/2017/jun/17/uber-drivers-homeless-assault-travis-kalanick.

18 Manyika, James, Susan Lund, Jacques Bughin, Kelsey Robinson, Jan Mischke, and Deepa Mahajan. *Independent Work: Choice, Necessity, and the Gig Economy*. McKinsey Global Institute. October 2016.

19 Kath, Ryan. Infamous TV Pitchman, Who Was Focus of 41 Action News Investigation, Ordered to Federal Court. KSHB Kansas City. March 7, 2013. https://www.kshb.com/news/local-news/investigations/infamous-tv-pitchman-who-was-focus-of-41-action-news-investigation-ordered-to-federal-court. And on *The Lookout*, see ABC News. Chasing the Dream Seller. *The Lookout*. May 29, 2013. http://abcnews.go.com/Nightline/video/part-chasing-dream-seller-19284233.

20 Kendall, Marisa. Uber Battling More Than 70 Lawsuits in Federal Courts. *Mercury News*. July 4, 2016. http://www.sfchronicle.com/business/article/Homejoy-Postmates-workers-sue-to-be-reclassified-6156533.php.

21 Irani, Lilly C., and M. Six Silberman. Turkopticon: Interrupting Worker Invisibility in Amazon Mechanical Turk. UC Irvine, Department of Informatics Bureau of Economic Interpretation. 2013.

22 Berg, Janine. Income Security in the On-Demand Economy: Findings and Policy Lessons from a Survey of Crowdworkers. International Labour Office. 2016. http://www.ilo.org/travail/whatwedo/publications/WCMS_479693/lang—en/index.htm.

23 Samasource. *Final Learnings Report to the Winthrop Rockefeller Foundation*. August 2017.

24 Wenzl, Tracy. How I Made over $1,000 on Upwork in My First Week. LinkedIn. March 16, 2016. https://www.linkedin.com/pulse/how-i-made-over-1000-upwork-my-first-week-tracy-wenzl/. And Jorgovan, Jake. How to Make $1,000+ per Week on Upwork. Jake

-Jorgovan.com. June 1, 2014. https://jake-jorgovan.com/blog/how
-to-make-1000-per-week-on-odesk.

25 Sundararajan, Arun. *The Sharing Economy*. MIT Press, 2016,
page 168.

26 Burke, Adrienne. Furloughed? Try Freelancing on Fiverr. Yahoo!
Small Business. https://smallbusiness.yahoo.com/advisor/blogs/profit
-minded/furloughed-try-freelancing-fiverr-145054277.html.

27 Fiverr press release. Fiverr Poll Says a Freelance Economy Works.
October 10, 2013. https://www.fiverr.com/news/economy_poll_work
_examiner.

28 Doleac, Jennifer L., and Luke C. D. Stein. The Visible Hand: Race
and Online Market Outcomes. *The Economic Journal*, vol. 123. November 2013. Pages F469–F492.

CHAPTER 9

1 Farr, Christina. Why Homejoy Failed. *Backchannel*. September 26, 2015. https://www.wired.com/2015/10/why-homejoy-failed
/#.3ifz7wf0m.

2 Q&A with Saman Rahmanian, CEO and Founder, Tischen.
StartupBeat. December 7, 2010. https://startupbeat.com/2010/12/qa
-with-saman-rahmanian-ceo-and-founder-tischen/.

3 Barack Obama speech on May 22, 2007, at The Electric Factory,
in Philadelphia, Pennsylvania.

4 Shontell, Alyson. Q Raises $775,000 from Bit-Time Angel Inves-
tors to Become a Godsend for Office Managers Everywhere. *Business Insider*. August 11, 2014. http://www.businessinsider.com/q
-raises-775000-to-make-cleaning-an-office-easy-to-schedule-and
-manage-2014-8.

5 Ton, Zeynep. *The Good Jobs Strategy: How the Smartest Compa-*

nies Invest in Employees to Lower Costs and Boost Profits. New Harvest, Houghton Mifflin Harcourt, 2014, pages vii, viii.

6 Ibid., page 73.

7 Griswold, Alison. Dirty Work. *Slate*. July 24, 2015. http://www .slate.com/articles/business/moneybox/2015/07/handy_a_hot _startup_for_home_cleaning_has_a_big_mess_of_its_own.html.

8 Ton, *The Good Jobs Strategy*, page 67.

9 Manjoo, Farhad. Start-Ups Finding the Best Employees Are Actually Employed. *New York Times*. June 24, 2015. https://www .nytimes.com/2015/06/25/technology/personaltech/start-ups -finding-the-best-employees-are-actually-employed.html?mtrref =www.google.com.

10 Reavis, Cate, and Zeynep Ton. Managed by Q. MIT Sloan School of Management, May 24, 2016, page 1. https://mitsloan.mit.edu /LearningEdge/operations-management/managedbyq/Pages /Managed-by-Q.aspx.

11 New York State Department of Labor. Occupational Wages. 2015.

12 Morea, Stephen. *Janitorial Service in the US*. IBISWorld Industry Report. August 2015.

13 Reavis and Ton, Managed by Q, page 6.

14 Ibid., page 8.

15 O'Brien, Ashley. Startup Banks $15M in Quest to Be "Best Employer." CNN. June 18, 2015. http://money.cnn.com/2015/06/18 /technology/managed-by-q-funding/index.html.

16 Li, Shan. Start-Up Washio Shuts Down. *Los Angeles Times*. August 30, 2016. http://www.latimes.com/business/la-fi-washio -startup-20160830-snap-story.html.

17 Cited in TrueBridge Capital Partners. The Gig Is Up: The Real

Value of Gig Economy Startups Isn't the Model—It's the Supply. *Forbes*. August 10, 2016. https://www.forbes.com/sites/truebridge /2016/08/10/the-real-value-of-gig-economy-startups/#1fafc0e4460c.

18 Kessler, Sarah. Why a New Generation of On-Demand Businesses Rejected the Uber Model. *Fast Company*. March 29, 2016. https://www.fastcompany.com/3058299/why-a-new-generation-of -on-demand-businesses-rejected-the-uber-model.

19 Gibbon, Kevin. Why Our Couriers Are No Longer Contractors. LinkedIn. July 1, 2015. https://www.linkedin.com/pulse/why-our -couriers-longer-contractors-kevin-gibbon/.

CHAPTER 10

1 Smiley, Lauren. The Shut-In Economy. *Matter*. March 25, 2015. https://medium.com/matter/the-shut-in-economy-ec3ec1294816.

2 Griswold, Alison. There's Still One Thing People Like about Uber. *Quartz*. June 8, 2017. https://qz.com/1000962/uber-is-a-mess-but-it -still-offers-a-great-ride-hailing-service/.

3 Camp, Garrett. Uber's Path Forward. *Medium*. June 20, 2017. https://medium.com/@gc/ubers-path-forward-b59ec9bd4ef6.

4 Email exchange with Ethan Pollack on December 16, 2017.

5 Campbell, Harry. What It's Like to Be at Uber's Mercy. *Splinter*. February 9, 2015. https://splinternews.com/what-its-like-to-be-at -ubers-mercy-1793845146.

6 In a blog post on *Medium,* Uber said that tips could be prone to personal bias and encourage drivers to spend time in wealthy neighborhoods. But also it thought customers didn't like tips. "Riders tell us that one of the things they like most about Uber is that it's hassle-free," the company wrote. "And that's how we intend to keep it." https://medium.com/uber-under-the-hood/our-approach -to-tipping-aa0074c0fddc.

7 Rideshare Dashboard. Uber Increases Minimum Fares in 20 Cities. August 31, 2016. http://ridesharedashboard.com/2016/08/31/uber-increases-minimum-fares-20-cities/.

8 Raile, Dan. The Medium Is the Movement: Abe Husein Is a Labor Leader for Our Times. *Pando*. October 21, 2015. https://pando.com/2015/10/21/medium-movement-abe-husein-labor-leader-our-times/.

9 Strike Planned: Some Uber Drivers to Stay Off Roads This Weekend. NBC Washington. October 17, 2015. http://www.nbcwashington.com/news/local/Uber-Strike-Some-Uber-Drivers-Plan-to-Stay-Off-Roads-This-Weekend-333219631.html.

10 Meyerson, Harold. The Forty-Year Slump. *American Prospect*. November 12, 2013. http://prospect.org/article/40-year-slump.

11 Abbruzzesse, Jason. Uber Drivers Plan a Three-Day National Strike to Call for Higher Fares. *Mashable*. October 16, 2015. http://mashable.com/2015/10/16/uber-driver-strike/#J9CNV2Tmfmq2.

12 Uber Newsroom. Beating the Winter Slump: Price Cuts for Riders and Guaranteed Fares for Drivers. January 9, 2016. https://newsroom.uber.com/beating-the-winter-slump-price-cuts-for-riders-and-guaranteed-earnings-for-drivers/.

13 Santora, Marc, and John Surico. Uber Drivers in New York City Protest Fare Cuts. *New York Times*. February 1, 2016. https://www.nytimes.com/2016/02/02/nyregion/uber-drivers-in-new-york-city-protest-fare-cuts.html?_r=3.

14 Alba, Davey. Angry Uber Drivers Threaten to Make a Mess of the Super Bowl. *Wired*. February 6, 2016. http://www.wired.com/2016/02/uber-drivers-protest-san-francisco-super-bowl/.

15 Alexander, Kurtis. Police Defuse Uber Protest Outside Super Bowl. *SFGate*. February 7, 2016. http://www.sfgate.com/bayarea/article/Police-defuse-Uber-protest-outside-Super-Bowl-6814223.php.

16 Fair Crowd Work. Ombuds Office for German Crowdsourcing Platforms Established. November 8, 2017. http://faircrowd.work/2017 /11/08/ombudsstelle-fuer-crowdworking-plattformen-vereinbart/.

17 Wiessner, Daniel, and Dan Levine. Uber Deal Shows Divide in Labor's Drive for Role in "Gig Economy." Reuters. May 23, 2016.

18 Scheiber, Noam, and Mike Isaac. Uber Recognizes New York Drivers' Group, Short of a Union. *New York Times*. May 10, 2016. https://www.nytimes.com/2016/05/11/technology/uber-agrees-to -union-deal-in-new-york.html.

19 Green, Carla, and Sam Levine. Homeless, Assaulted, Broke: Drivers Left behind as Uber Promises Change at the Top. *The Guardian*. June 17, 2017. https://www.theguardian.com/us-news /2017/jun/17/uber-drivers-homeless-assault-travis-kalanick.

20 Salehi, Niloufar, Lilly Irani, Michael S. Bernstein, Ali Alkhatib, Eva Ogbe, Kristy Milland, and Clickhappier. We Are Dynamo: Overcoming Stalling and Friction in Collective Action for Crowd Workers. Paper presented at the meeting of the CHI. 2015.

21 Bohannon, John. Psychologists Grow Increasingly Dependent on Online Research Subjects. *Science Magazine*. June 7, 2016. http:// www.sciencemag.org/news/2016/06/psychologists-grow-increa singly-dependent-online-research-subjects.

22 Pörtner, Claus C., Nail Hassairi, and Michael Toomin. Only If You Pay Me More: Field Experiments Support Compensating Wage Differentials Theory. Working paper. October 2015. http://static1 .squarespace.com/static/53c31c5ce4b053fc7d131b18/t/56405d98e4b07 bcd9d9704a1/1447058840358/Portner+-+compensating+wage+diffe rentials.pdf.

23 Salehi et al. We Are Dynamo.

24 Harris, Mark. Amazon Mechanical Turk Workers Protest: "I Am a Human Being, Not an Algorithm." *The Guardian*. December 3,

2014. https://www.theguardian.com/technology/2014/dec/03/amazon
-mechanical-turk-workers-protest-jeff-bezos.

[25] Katz, Miranda. Amazon's Turker Crowd Has Had Enough. *Wired.* August 23, 2017. https://www.wired.com/story/amazons
-turker-crowd-has-had-enough/.

[26] The traditional unions that once helped create the American middle class have nowhere near as much influence today as they once did. Only about 11% of the workforce (and just 6.6% of the non-government workforce) belonged to a union in 2016, compared to about 20% in 1983 (US Bureau of Labor Statistics. Union membership as a percentage of employed wage and salary workers), and the growing group of independent workers like Kristy, Curtis, Abe, and Terrence's students fall outside of union organizing rights altogether. Dynamo was not the only idea for how to organize these workers outside of the traditional union system.

A website called Coworker attempted to create online groups of workers and help them petition their employers. Starbucks employees used it to campaign for a policy change that allowed for visible tattoos and went on to win wage increases, scheduling improvements, and changes to parental leave policies. (Horovitz, Bruce. Tattoos, Nose Studs OK for Starbucks Baristas. *USA Today.* October 16, 2014. https://www.usatoday.com/story/money/business/2014
/10/16/starbucks-tattoos-nose-studs-baristas-dress-code/1736
9455/.)

The National Domestic Workers Alliance, a worker advocacy group, organized nannies, elder caretakers, home cleaners, and other domestic workers, all of whom tended to be independent contractors. Instead of union dues, the organization mostly ran on grants.

A non-traditional union founded in 2003, called the Freelancers Union, advocated for another form of support for independent workers. It partnered with insurance companies on dental, life, and disability insurance plans sold to freelancers, as well as a retirement plan. It also ran two medical clinics in New York for members of its insurance plan, which provided access to unlimited primary care with a $0 co-pay and free acupuncture, nutritional counseling, yoga, Tai Chi classes, and stress-management programs. The idea was that, as with the AARP and Planned Parenthood, services would attract members and fund advocacy work.

None of these efforts could grow as quickly as companies backed by millions (sometimes billions) of dollars in venture capital. But they were a start.

CHAPTER 11

1 Katz, Lawrence F., and Alan B. Krueger. The Rise and Nature of Alternative Work Arrangements in the United States, 1995–2015. National Bureau of Economic Research Working Paper 22667. 2016. http://www.nber.org/papers/w22667.

2 *Good Work: The Taylor Review of Modern Working Practices*. Department for Business, Energy & Industrial Strategy. July 2017. https://www.gov.uk/government/publications/good-work-the -taylor-review-of-modern-working-practices.

3 Center for Retirement Research at Boston College. Frequently Requested Data. Workers with Pension Coverage by Type of Plan, 1983, 1992, 2001, and 2013. http://crr.bc.edu/wp-content/uploads/1012 /01/figure-15.pdf.

4 401(k) plans are employer-sponsored retirement savings accounts in which employees can contribute pay before it's taxed. Some employers, but not all, match some portion of the contributions that employees make to these accounts.

5 Munnell, Alicia H., and Mauricio Soto. The Outlook for Pension Contributions and Profits. *U.S. Journal of Pension Economics and Finance*, vol. 3, no. 1. 2004. Presumably, over time, wages will rise to make up the difference, but when a group of researchers at Bos-

ton College looked at a group of otherwise healthy companies that had frozen their pension plans—including Coca-Cola, IBM, Verizon, and Hewlett-Packard—they determined savings were the biggest motivation. "The logic must be that cutting pensions will cause less commotion than cutting cash wages," they wrote.

6 Bureau of Labor Statistics News Release. Employee Benefits in the United States—March 2017. July 21, 2017.

7 A high number of graduates looking for work, but not eligible for unemployment benefits, and people who have been unemployed longer than the maximum amount of time allowed contributed, but also, nine states cut back on the 26-week duration. North Carolina cut it down to 14 weeks. McHugh, Rick, and Will Kimball. How Long Can We Go? State Unemployment Insurance Programs Exclude Record Numbers of Jobless Workers. Economic Policy Institute. Briefing Paper #392. March 9, 2015.

8 Berg, Janine. Income Security in the On-Demand Economy: Findings and Policy Lessons from a Survey of Crowdworkers. International Labour Office. 2016.

9 Kaiser Family Foundation. 2015 Employer Health Benefits Survey.

10 Ibid.

11 Bureau of Labor Statistics. Employee Benefits Survey. March 2015. https://www.bls.gov/ncs/ebs/benefits/2015/ownership/civilian/table09a.htm.

12 Is the Affordable Care Act Working? New York Times. Interactive article produced by Troy Griggs, Haeyoun Park, Alicia Parlapiano, Sona Patel, Karl Russell, and R. Smith. https://www.nytimes.com/interactive/2014/10/27/us/is-the-affordable-care-act-working.html?_r=1#/uninsured.

13 Dynan, Karen, Douglas Elmendorf, and Daniel Sichel. The Evolution of Household Income Volatility. B.E. Journal of Economic Analysis & Policy. December 18, 2012. https://www.degruyter.com

/view/j/bejeap.2012.12.issue-2/1935-1682.3347/1935-1682.3347.xml
?format=INT.

14 Federal Reserve Board. *Report on the Economic Well-Being of US Households*. July 2014.

15 Gosselin, Peter G. If America Is Richer, Why Are Its Families So Much Less Secure? *Los Angeles Times*. October 10, 2004. http://www.latimes.com/news/la-fi-riskshift10oct10-story.html.

16 Hanauer, Nick, and David Rolf. Shared Security, Shared Growth. *Democracy*, no. 37. Summer 2015. http://democracyjournal.org/magazine/37/shared-security-shared-growth/.

17 Board of Governors of the Federal Reserve. *Report on the Economic Well-Being of U.S. Households in 2015*. May 2016.

18 Economists generally agree that in the long term, businesses pass their share of payroll taxes onto employees by paying lower wages. If they're asked to pay 7% of wages to fund retirement payments and other social programs, for instance, they'll reduce worker pay by 7%. In this scenario, the worker fares the same either way. But as it plays out in the real world, employers hesitate to cut wages immediately, so workers benefit from the increased commitment of employers to pay into social programs in the short term and possibly longer, if the decrease in pay would make the job uncompetitive. Portable benefits, however they were structured, seemed to many like the best chance to support workers without traditional jobs. As Ethan Pollack, the associate director of research and policy at the Aspen Institute, explains it: "If you mandated a 25% contribution [from employers], worker payments would likely not immediately go down by 25%. Now, the fact that they are contractors rather than [employees] probably means that the wages are less sticky, and therefore will adjust downward somewhat in the near term. But it's unlikely they'll adjust downward by the full 25%. So in the near term, businesses will share in the burden."

19 Kessler, Sarah. US Senator Mark Warner Proposed a $20 Million

Fund to Experiment with Portable Benefits for Freelancers and Gig Economy Workers. *Quartz.* May 25, 2017. https://qz.com/991270 /us-senator-mark-warner-proposed-a-20-million-fund-to -experiment-with-portable-benefits-for-freelancers-gig-economy -workers-and-contractors/.

[20] Mccabe, David, and Tim Devaney. Hillary Clinton's Uber Problem. *The Hill.* July 24, 2015. http://thehill.com/business-a-lobbying /248999-hillary-clintons-uber-problem.

[21] Remarks by Senator Elizabeth Warren. Strengthening the Basic Bargain for Workers in the Modern Economy. New America Annual Conference. May 19, 2016. https://www.warren.senate.gov/files /documents/2016-5-19_Warren_New_America_Remarks.pdf.

[22] Grenoble, Ryan. Elizabeth Warren Takes on Uber, Lyft and the "Gig Economy." *Huffington Post.* May 19, 2016.

[23] Hoover, Amanda. Elizabeth Warren Calls for Increased Regulations on Uber, Lyft, and the "Gig Economy." Boston.com. May 19, 2016. https://www.boston.com/news/politics/2016/05/19/elizabeth -warren-calls-increased-regulations-uber-lyft-gig-economy.

[24] Jopson, Barney, and Leslie Hook. Elizabeth Warren Slams Uber and Lyft. *Financial Times.* May 19, 2016. https://www.ft.com /content/abc00336-1de1-11e6-b286-cddde55ca122.

[25] Trottman, Melanie. Employees vs. Independent Contractors: U.S. Weighs in on Debate over How to Classify Workers. *The Wall Street Journal.* July 15, 2015. https://www.wsj.com/articles/labor-department -releases-guidance-on-classification-of-workers-1436954401.

[26] Kreider, Benjamin. Risk Shift and the Gig Economy. Economic Policy Institute's *Working Economic Blog.* August 4, 2015. http:// www.epi.org/blog/risk-shift-and-the-gig-economy/.

[27] Mishel, Lawrence. Uber Is Not the Future of Work. *The Atlantic.* November 16, 2015. https://www.theatlantic.com/business /archive/2015/11/uber-is-not-the-future-of-work/415905/.

28 The American Presidency Project. 706—Remarks at a White House Summit on Worker Voice Question-and-Answer Session. October 7, 2015.

29 Perez, Tom. Innovation and the Contingent Workforce. *Department of Labor Blog.* January 25, 2016.

30 Borzi, Phyllis. Keynote Address at the Retirement Security in the On-Demand Economy. The Aspen Institute. April 11, 2016.

31 Harris, S., and A. Krueger. A Proposal for Modernizing Labor Laws for Twenty-First-Century Work: The "Independent Worker." The Hamilton Project. Discussion Paper 2015–10. December 2015. http://www.hamiltonproject.org/assets/files/modernizing_labor _laws_for_twenty_first_century_work_krueger_harris.pdf.

32 Koopman, John. Zen and the Art of Uber Driving. *Fast Company.* July 14, 2016. http://www.fastcoexist.com/3061620/zen-and -the-art-of-uber-driving.

33 Harris and Krueger, Proposal for Modernizing Labor Laws.

34 AFL-CIO press release. AFL-CIO Asserts That Gig Economy Workers Are Employees. March 1, 2016. https://aflcio.org/press /releases/afl-cio-asserts-gig-economy-workers-are-employees.

35 Johnston, Chris. Uber Drivers Win Key Employment Case. BBC. October 28, 2016. http://www.bbc.com/news/business-37802386.

36 A 2017 UK government review of employment practices in the gig economy did suggest the third category, however, has resulted in more good than harm for workers. It recommended that the government clarify and enforce the criteria for the in-between classification, not eliminate it all together.

37 Hanauer and Rolf, Shared Security, Shared Growth.

38 US Department of Labor press release. US Labor Department Announces Availability of Grants to Develop Portable Retirement Savings Plans for Low-Wage Workers. July 27, 2016.

CHAPTER 12

[1] Juno Is Growing. Uber People.net. https://uberpeople.net/threads/juno-refer-a-driver-get-a-bonus.92609/.

[2] The book is called *Ours to Hack and to Own: The Rise of Platform Cooperativism, A New Vision for the Future of Work and a Fairer Internet.*

[3] Holmberg, Susan. Fighting Short-Termism with Worker Power. The Roosevelt Institute. October 2017.

[4] Holmberg, Susan. Want to Fix US Corporations? Put Regular Workers on Company Boards. *Quartz.* October 23, 2017. https://work.qz.com/1106972/want-to-fix-us-corporations-put-regular-workers-on-company-boards/.

[5] Cortese, Amy. A New Wrinkle in the Gig Economy: Workers Get Most of the Money. *New York Times.* July 20, 2016. https://www.nytimes.com/2016/07/21/business/smallbusiness/a-new-wrinkle-in-the-gig-economy-workers-get-most-of-the-money.html?_r=0.

[6] Scholz, Trebor, and Nathan Schneider. The People's Uber: Why the Sharing Economy Must Share Ownership. *Fast Company.* October 7, 2015. https://www.fastcompany.com/3051845/the-peoples-uber-why-the-sharing-economy-must-share-ownership.

[7] Feeding America. Food Insecurity in the United States. http://map.feedingamerica.org/county/2015/overall/arkansas/county/desha.

[8] Blanchflower, David G., and Andrew J. Oswald. What Makes an Entrepreneur? *Journal of Labor Economics*, vol. 16, no. 1. 1998. Pages 26–60. https://ssrn.com/abstract=1505204.

[9] Carr, Michael, and Emily Wiemers. The Decline in Lifetime Earnings Mobility in the US: Evidence from Survey-Linked Administrative Data. Working Paper. September 2016.

10 Semuels, Alana. Poor at 20, Poor for Life. *The Atlantic*. July 14, 2016. https://www.theatlantic.com/business/archive/2016/07/social -mobility-america/491240/.

CHAPTER 13

1 Bercovici, Jeff. Why Handy Chose a Painful Path to Profitability. *Inc.* November 2016.

2 US Bureau of Labor Statistics. Employment, Hours, and Earnings from the Current Employment Statistics Survey (National).

3 Farrell, Diana, and Fiona Greig. The Online Platform Economy: Has Growth Peaked? JP Morgan Chase Institute. November 2016.

4 Kessler, Sarah. The Gig Economy Is Also a Management Style. *Quartz*. January 17, 2017. https://qz.com/862319/the-gig-economy -is-also-a-management-style/.

5 70%: Manyika, James, Susan Lund, Jacques Bughin, Kelsey Robinson, Jan Mischke, and Deepa Mahajan. *Independent Work: Choice, Necessity, and the Gig Economy*. McKinsey Global Institute. October 2016. 80%: Wartzman, Rick. Working in the Gig Economy Is Both Desirable and Detestable. *Fortune*. April 27, 2016. http://fortune .com/2016/04/27/uber-gig-economy/. 85%: Wartzman, Rick. Working in the Gig Economy Is Both Desirable and Detestable. *Fortune*. April 27, 2016. http://fortune.com/2016/04/27/uber-gig-economy/.

6 Wartzman, Working in the Gig Economy.

7 Oisin, Hanrahan. We Must Protect the On-Demand Economy to Protect the Future of Work. *Wired*. November 9, 2015. https://www .wired.com/2015/11/we-must-protect-the-on-demand-economy -to-protect-the-future-of-work/.

8 Lyft Blog. Lyft × Honest Dollar: Introducing Savings and Retire-ment Solutions for Lyft Drivers. November 19, 2015. https://blog .lyft.com/posts/lyft-x-honest-dollar.

[9] Bureau of Labor Statistics. National Compensation Survey: Employee Benefits in the United States, March 2014. September 2014.

EPILOGUE

[1] Press release. Workers and US Government Cheated Out of Billions in Stolen Wages and Lost Tax Revenue. National Employment Law Project. February 19, 2014.

[2] Newton, Casey. Uber Will Eventually Replace All of Its Drivers with Self-Driving Cars. *The Verge*. May 28, 2014. https://hbr.org/2017/07/lots-of-employees-get-misclassified-as-contractors-heres-why-it-matters.

[3] Kessler, Sarah. A Timeline of When Self-Driving Vehicles Will Be on the Road, According to the People Making Them. *Quartz*. March 29, 2017. https://qz.com/943899/a-timeline-of-when-self-driving-cars-will-be-on-the-road-according-to-the-people-making-them/.

[4] McKinsey Global Institute. What the Future of Work Will Mean for Jobs, Skills, and Wages. November 2017. https://www.mckinsey.com/global-themes/future-of-organizations-and-work/what-the-future-of-work-will-mean-for-jobs-skills-and-wages.

[5] Lynley, Matthew. Travis Kalanick Says Uber Has 40 Million Monthly Users. *TechCrunch*. October 19, 2016. https://techcrunch.com/2016/10/19/travis-kalanick-says-uber-has-40-million-monthly-active-riders/.

[6] Quoted in Dray, Philip. *There Is Power in a Union*. Anchor Books, 2010, page 248.

Index